RANGERS
OFFICIAL
ALL-TIME GREATS

Douglas Russell

Lomond Books
A Grange Publication

g Published by Grange Communications Ltd., Edinburgh, under licence from Rangers Football Club plc.

Printed in the EU.

Photographs supplied by D. C. Thomson & Co. Ltd.

ISBN: 1-84204-000-6

CONTENTS

INTRODUCTION

Much of the lifeblood of football is history and legend. From one part of the country to another, every major football club has its own story, littered with famous names from its own illustrious past.

Over the years, since those four youths (brothers Peter and Moses McNeil, Peter Campbell and William McBeath) shared a common goal way back in 1872, Glasgow Rangers has had more than its fair share of great and heroic players, outstanding teams and wonderful occasions.

The story of Rangers Football Club is well documented and it is not the purpose of this book to cover that same ground. Although numerous famous (and indeed some infamous and some less well-known) events are, naturally, touched upon, the real emphasis here is on a selection of those players who carried the very real hopes and aspirations of many while wearing the blue.

Covering both themselves and the club in glory, they were all reborn as Ibrox heroes in the eyes of the supporters. In due course, and with the passage of time, some exceptional cases would evolve into legends.

Some players, becoming heroes on the basis of just one game, then see their brief shining light extinguished by an almost immediate fall from grace.

Others develop heroic status over a period time (months or even years), in many cases after an inauspicious start. Legends, on the other hand, are a different breed altogether. Immortals of such rare vintage that their deeds, with the passing of the decades, have become almost mythical.

Comparison with the exploits of Ulysses, Agamemnon and the other Greek warriors would somehow not seem out of place!

From Jerry Dawson to Chris Woods, Jim Baxter to Jorg Albertz, Willie Thornton to Mark Hateley and Willie Waddell to Davie Cooper. Names that carry the same luminous blue signature.

From Alan Morton and Davie Meiklejohn in the 1920s, Bob McPhail and Torry Gillick in the 1930s, George Young and Willie Woodburn in the 1940s, Alex Scott and Billy Simpson in the 1950s, John Greig and Jim Forrest in the 1960s, Sandy Jardine and Tommy McLean in the 1970s, Ally McCoist and Ian Durrant in the 1980s, through to Andy Goram and Stuart McCall in the 1990s.

Names written in blue for all time. Whether goalkeepers, defenders, midfielders, strikers or wingers, there is one common link . . . they are all worthy of a place in the Ibrox Hall of Fame.

Rangers men through and through, this is their story . . . and their glory!

DEREK JOHNSTONE

Few players excel with Rangers in more than one position. Derek Johnstone is one of a rare breed, having worn the blue to notable effect at centre-forward, centre-half as well as in midfield.

After signing as a schoolboy in 1968, the big lad turned professional in July 1970. In September of that year, he scored twice on his senior debut against Cowdenbeath at Ibrox in the league. One month later, Derek Johnstone's name was on everyone's lips. Outjumping defenders McNeill and Craig, his headed goal in the League Cup Final victory over Celtic was witnessed by a crowd of 106,000 and is now the very stuff of legend. Not quite seventeen years of age, Johnstone became the youngest player to score the winning goal in a cup final. Of greater importance was the fact that Rangers had just won their first major trophy in more than four years.

An impressive medal collection comprises three League Championships (1975, 1976 and 1978), five Scottish Cups (1973, 1976, 1978, 1979 and 1981) and five League Cups in Seasons 1970/71, 1975/76, 1977/78, 1978/79 and 1981/82. Naturally, there is also a European Cup Winners' Medal of 1972, when he replaced the injured Colin Jackson at the heart of the defence for the game in Barcelona.

It is certainly worth noting that 'DJ' not only scored as a centre-forward and centre-half in separate Scottish Cup Finals but also won Scottish Cup Medals with Rangers in three different positions - the two aforementioned plus midfield!

Although Johnstone was an integral part of Rangers 'treble-winning' teams of 1976 and 1978, netting 27 and 38 times respectively, it is an encounter outwith this period that is often recalled by supporters. The player (along with Davie Cooper and John MacDonald) was dropped for the Scottish Cup Final against Dundee United in 1981. Following a drawn, no-scoring affair, all three were reinstated for the replay and a superb 'Light Blue' performance which left the Taysiders reeling. The trophy was won on a 4-1 scoreline.

Chelsea paid £30,000 for his services in 1983. Although Jock Wallace brought the player back to Ibrox in January 1985, the arrival of Graeme Souness finally ended his Rangers career.

Derek Johnstone will always be remembered for his versatility - not only as a deadly finisher but also as a magnificent stopper in the centre of the defence.

Rangers Career Statistics
Games : 546 Goals : 210 League Championship Medals : 3
Scottish Cup Medals : 5 League Cup Medals : 5
European : 1

JORG ALBERTZ

Some goals are just that 'wee' bit special. Cast your thoughts back to a bitter January night in 1997, when Celtic came calling on league duty.

Rangers had pushed forward early in the game and David Robertson was tripped by McNamara after taking a short Gascoigne pass. As the resultant free-kick was some thirty yards from goal, the 'Gers had obviously more than one option as both 'Gazza' and Jorg Albertz considered the possibilities. The German decided to go for goal. With Celtic's five-man defensive wall in place, Jorg strode forward to unleash a killer strike that flew past McNamara at the end of the wall. 'Keeper Kerr really had no chance and was comprehensively beaten as the ball buried itself in the corner of the bulging net at the Broomloan end, recording a maximum speed of 79.8 miles per hour on route!

In the eyes of the Rangers fans, even before this spectacular strike, midfielder Albertz was 'one of them'. Since his arrival from Hamburg (where he was club captain) for Season 1996/97, a special relationship had been formed. In that first year, Jorg scored in five consecutive games, beginning 'away' to Hearts in December (4-1 victory), followed by Raith Rovers (4-0 at 'home'), Celtic as mentioned, Hibernian (2-1 at Easter Road) and the 4-0 drubbing of Aberdeen at Ibrox in January 1997. 'The Hammer' had made his mark on the road to 'Nine-in-a-Row'.

Despite the fact that the player had his critics the next season, his contribution was still vital. Several important strikes included the late, late winner at Easter Road (February 1998), when his twenty-five yard shot arced over Bryan Gunn and dipped into the net. Of course, this was nothing compared to the German's two stunning goals against Celtic, two weeks in a row in April, that helped secure famous wins:-

Venue No.1 (Parkhead and the Scottish Cup Semi-Final) witnessed a vintage solo effort with only two minutes remaining. Gathering a loose ball just inside his own half, Jorg moved purposefully forward as the green rearguard retreated. Past the shadowing Lambert and into the penalty area, where an unstoppable left-foot shot sent the travelling Rangers support into raptures. Venue No.2 (Ibrox and the League) was, in many ways, a re-run of the previous week's scenario, only this time his tracker was Burley. The outcome was, however, just the same.

With the arrival of Dick Advocaat for Season 1998/99, there were changes aplenty on (and off) the park but Albertz continued to endear himself to the Rangers faithful. Apart from scoring the winner in the League Cup Final (2-1 v. St. Johnstone, 29.11.98) and an impressive 'hat-trick' against Dundee in February, another of his amazing strikes almost took the 'Light Blues' past Parma in the UEFA Cup tie in Italy.

On that highly charged May day in 1999, when Rangers secured the Championship in the Parkhead cauldron, it was the coolest man on the park who stepped forward to famously convert the most important penalty of the year.

The Iceman........Jorg Albertz.

Rangers Career Statistics
League Championship Medals : 2 Scottish Cup Medals : 1
League Cup Medals : 2

McEWAN'S
LAGER

TERRY BUTCHER

And in the beginning, there was Terry Butcher. The towering six-foot, four-inch deputy captain of England, with the formidable reputation, arrived at Ibrox in August 1986 to become, in many ways, the focal point, of that new era under Graeme Souness. Certainly, he would prove to be one of Rangers most valuable signings of modern times.

By the end of October, the League Cup was destined for the Trophy Room after Terry had led his men to a 2-1 final victory over Celtic. But the best was yet to come, some six months later, in May. Although it was only the 'big man's' second goal of the season, it was enough to secure the required point at Pittodrie and Rangers' first title win in nine long years. Throughout the campaign, Butcher's defence had only conceded twenty-three league goals compared to forty-five the previous season, before his timely arrival in the country.

The player was shown the 'red card' during that contentious 'Old Firm' clash in October 1987, when two others, Chris Woods and Frank McAvennie, also headed for an early bath. Worse was to follow exactly one month later. During the Ibrox clash with Aberdeen, he broke his leg in a challenge with Alex McLeish. Some would suggest that Rangers' Championship hopes perished at the same time.

Back in action for the next year's campaign, life for both defender and club returned to winning normality, with a League and League Cup 'double' being toasted in Govan. Season 1989/90 and Tannadice in April was the place and month that confirmed Championship No.40 for the 'Light Blues'. In thirty-six games, only a miserly nineteen goals had been given away.

By now, it was nigh on impossible to visualise that Rangers rearguard without the inspirational Butcher at its core but prior to the League Cup Semi-Final of 1990, the impossible became reality. After falling out with the manager, the player was literally sent to Coventry and signed for the Midlands club. It was, indeed, a sad end to his career in Scotland.

To this day, however, Terry Butcher holds a special place in the hearts of all 'Follow-Followers', as an Englishman who became a 'True Blue'.

Rangers Career Statistics
Games: 176 Goals: 11 League Championship Medals: 3
League Cup Medals: 2

McEWAN'S
LAGER

DAVIE COOPER

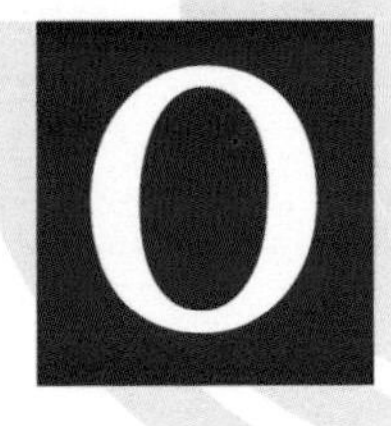

ne of the Light Blues' most favoured and gifted sons, the supremely talented winger (with a left-foot that could do almost anything!) signed from Clydebank in June 1977 for £100,000 after starring for the 'Bankies' in three League Cup ties against Rangers the previous season. By 6 May the following year, Rangers were toasting a domestic 'treble', with the influential Cooper having started in all but two games throughout the season. He also claimed his first 'Old Firm' strike in the 2-1 March League Cup Final victory.

In the Drybrough Cup Final of August 1979 at Hampden, Davie scored one of the greatest goals ever seen at the old stadium, juggling past four mesmerised Celtic defenders before netting in his team's 3-1 triumph. Finals of Cups seemed to bring out the best in him. To cite but two examples:

a) the quite ferocious free-kick in the League Cup Final of 1987 that Aberdeen's Jim Leighton just managed to get a hand to......on the way back out!
b) the stunning performance against Dundee United in the 1981 Scottish Cup Final replay, when he tore the heart and soul from a tangerine rearguard incapable of stopping him.

More often than not, people commented that if 'Coop' was on form, then so were Rangers, such was his importance to the club. Surprisingly, for someone with so much talent, the winger only played for his country on twenty-two occasions.

When Graeme Souness' team lifted that 'first' Championship in May 1987, Davie missed just two games in the entire campaign. With appearances declining over the next couple of years, however, the player joined Motherwell in 1989 and enjoyed a new lease of life, producing many vintage performances for the Lanarkshire outfit. Then, in 1993, he returned to his first club, Clydebank and the circle was complete.

The tragic news that Davie Cooper had passed away on 23 March 1995 (following a brain haemorrhage the day before) tore a hole in the hearts of thousands. And not just followers of the blue. First and foremost a Rangers man, Davie Cooper was (and always will be) a major part of the club and its history. In a very special sense, he had never really left Ibrox.

Rangers Career Statistics
Games: 540   Goals: 75   League Championship Medals: 3
Scottish Cup Medals: 3   League Cup Medals: 7

IAN DURRANT

Certain days have a darkness about them, regardless of the weather. Friends of Rangers need no reminding that 8 October 1988 was a black day at Pittodrie Stadium, Aberdeen.

Govan boy, Ian Durrant, joined the only team he ever wanted to play for as a schoolboy. Benefiting from the Rangers training and coaching system, he made his league debut in the 'away' game against Morton in April 1985. By the following season, a blossoming Durrant, now established in the first team, was scoring on his 'Old Firm' debut at Ibrox, when visitors, Celtic, were comprehensively beaten 3-0.

With the arrival of Graeme Souness, the No.10 jersey would virtually become his own. Ian wore it with pride on no fewer than 39 occasions throughout that first Championship year. The League Cup also returned to the Trophy Room after Durrant's opening strike in the final set Rangers on the road to a 2-1 victory over the team from Glasgow's East End.

Although the title was not retained in Season 1987/88, the League Cup did remain at Ibrox. Rangers faced Aberdeen at Hampden in October 1987 in what was to prove one of the great finals of the modern era and, indeed, it was on this day that probably the most enduring image of Ian Durrant was captured for all time. After the 'Dons' opened the scoring, goals from Davie Cooper (a really quite ferocious free-kick) and our hero gave the 'Light Blues' the lead. The team from the north then scored twice before Robert Fleck's dramatic late, late equaliser. With no further scoring in extra time, it was all down to penalties. Who can ever forget Durrant, arms high in 'Victory V' celebration, after he had netted the decisive kick? That priceless image is now frozen in the mind.

So, to Pittodrie, in the third month of the 1988/89 Championship, when, following a horrendously shocking tackle by Neil Simpson, his right knee was virtually shattered. It would be almost three long and painful years before Ian pulled on his beloved blue again. But he did, indeed, return and on that day at Ibrox, against Hibernian in April 1991, thirty-five thousand people rose as one to greet him, emerging from the darkness into sunlight once again.

Season 1992/93 was just a 'wee' bit special for both player and team at home and abroad, with a domestic 'treble' here and unqualified success in Europe. Most will remember Durrant's stunning equaliser against Marseille in the hostile atmosphere of the Velodrome, ensuring that Rangers became the first visitors in 15 European ties to avoid defeat there.

This was the brave midfielder's third goal in the unforgettable European Cup campaign, his other strikes being the away goal against Danish Champions, Lyngby (in the September first-round match) and his club's opening goal against Bruges of Belgium in March '93. No doubt 'Durranty' would also remind us that it was from his corner kick that Leeds 'keeper, John Lukic, punched the ball into his own net to equalise against the English Champions during that memorable 'Battle of Britain' first-leg at Ibrox. The season culminated in his 'Man of the Match' award for a peerless performance in the treble-clinching 1993 Scottish Cup Final victory over Aberdeen.

The memories remain many and that abiding image of Ian Durrant, arms aloft in 'Victory V' celebration after scoring, is now part of Ibrox folklore.

Rangers Career Statistics

Games: 347 Goals: 45 League Championship Medals: 3
ScottishCup Medals: 3 League Cup Medals: 4

McEWAN'S
LAGER

IAN FERGUSON

Even as a youngster, there was only ever one team for him and the view of Parkhead from his boyhood home in the East End of Glasgow meant absolutely nothing. Indeed, throughout an Ibrox playing career which now spans more than a decade, it has often been said that Ian Ferguson's beating heart pumps only blue blood through the dark blue veins of his body, such is the midfielder's commitment to the Rangers cause. Although this 'fact' may just be the slightest of exaggerations, few players of the modern era have worn the jersey with so much pride. Some, in truth, to greater acclaim but few with greater pride.

It was Graeme Souness who brought him to the club in February 1988, with approximately £1 million moving just a short distance along the M8 as the agreed transfer fee with St. Mirren. The previous year, Ferguson had famously scored the winning goal for the Paisley outfit in the Scottish Cup Final when favourites Dundee United were beaten in the Hampden clash. The Taysiders were the opponents again for his opening game in the blue (1-1, 27.2.88), with his first goal coming some six weeks later during the 2-3 'away' league defeat at the hands of Morton in Greenock.

Ferguson was simply immense the following year (1988/89), playing in forty-three games with thirteen strikes to his credit in both domestic and European competition. For good measure, he scored with a spectacular scissors kick in the 3-2 League Cup Final victory over Aberdeen in late October. Indeed, it was goals from Fergie, in consecutive seasons, that finally ended not only their Championship aspirations (2-0, 30.3.93) but also the League Cup involvement (2-1, 1.9.93) of the team from the Granite City. Although injury and illness both took their toll over the years, Ian played his 300th game for Rangers when the 'Light Blues' travelled to Tannadice on the last day of the league campaign in May 1988. Along the way, he had collected nine League, two Scottish Cup and four League Cup medals, with another three, of course, due to come his way in Advocaat's historic 'treble' of 1998/99.

Many friends of the club still recall, with some relish, the pre-season challenge game match in the summer of 1989 when 'Gazza' (then wearing the white of Tottenham Hotspur) was literally played off the park by Fergie. His midfield performance that warm August day was quite masterly. Just over nine years later, following the 'Light Blues' 1-1 draw with Parma in the UEFA Cup, one Italian newspaper singled him out for special attention and commented that he had 'destroyed Veron (their brilliant Argentinian playmaker) in the first-half and kept Rangers' engine running throughout.'

When the team secured its glorious 'hat-trick' of triumphs at Hampden on 29 May, 1999, no one reacted more quickly than Ferguson following Rod Wallace's winner in the Scottish Cup Final. He was off the bench celebrating before the ball had even hit the back of the net! That reaction, in many ways, really sums up the player: a Rangers man . . . through and through.

Rangers Career Statistics
League Championship Medals : 10 Scottish Cup Medals : 3
League Cup Medals : 5

ntl:

WILLIE HENDERSON

Any student knows there were huge contrasts this century between the austere fifties and subsequent swinging sixties. Yet, in a most peculiar way, there was really little between them as, in each period, a supremely talented (but different) right-winger wore the blue of Rangers.

The 'boy wonder', Willie Henderson, succeeded the great fifties sensation, Alex Scott, at Ibrox. 'Boy wonder?' Well, he was a schoolboy international before making his Rangers debut at seventeen (in the 2-1 league victory over Clyde, March 1961) and then, just prior to his nineteenth birthday, won the first of 29 Scotland 'Caps'. In modern times, only Denis Law pulled on the dark blue at an earlier age.

Fast, strong, an expert dribbler and superb crosser (strikers Ralph Brand and Jimmy Millar benefited the most), the 'Wee Barra' was a joy to behold - all five feet and four inches of him could not be contained, even by a posse of defenders. In the second game of Season 1962/63, he scored the only and decisive goal against Celtic at Parkhead, as Rangers began a Championship-winning campaign, with the Scottish Cup also being celebrated that year. The winger (who was short-sighted and wore contact lenses when playing) would go on to collect two League titles, four Scottish Cups and two League Cups in his Ibrox career.

In Europe, he was part of the team that fell at the final Nuremberg hurdle in 1967. Earlier in the same Cup Winners' Cup competition, Willie had netted the winner against Slavia Sofia in the semi-final, second leg tie (1-0, 3.5.67).

Following a domestic 'treble' in Season 1963/64, a famous bunion operation meant that he missed sixteen of the thirty-four league games next time round. Rangers did not retain their Championship and it would be eleven extremely long years before that particular trophy returned to Ibrox. Henderson was a contemporary of Celtic's Jimmy Johnstone and, with the Parkhead side beginning their own 'Nine-in-a-Row' sequence in 1965/66, more of the spotlight naturally shifted to his counterpart.

The winger joined Sheffield Wednesday in July 1972. Then it was on to Hong Kong Rangers and finally back to Scotland with Airdrie.

Willie Henderson was one of the true, genuine characters of the Scottish game, whose joyous enthusiasm and style is sadly lacking in today's modern game. The Rangers support just loved him. Not everybody can say that.

Rangers Career Statistics
Games: 426 Goals: 62 League Championship Medals: 2
Scottish Cup Medals: 4 League Cup Medals: 2

PAUL GASCOIGNE

here were many raised eyebrows in the summer of 1995, when manager Walter Smith announced that Rangers had completed the signing of wayward genius, Paul Gascoigne, from 'Serie A' club, Lazio, for £4.3 million. His pedigree was never in doubt, just the fact that the Geordie had only played 47 games in three seasons in Italy, having spent a fair percentage of time on the injury list. Any lingering doubts were soon quashed, however, and the player hit a rich vein of form on the park, becoming an instant folk hero to the legions in blue.

In his first season in Glasgow, Gascoigne netted nineteen times in forty-one games, including a quite sublime goal against Celtic at Parkhead, when he ran the length of the park (2-0, 30.9.95). Probably three of his most celebrated strikes came in the Championship decider against Aberdeen in late April - his second that day being rightly judged as one of the finest individual efforts ever seen at Ibrox. With barely ten minutes remaining and the score tied at 1-1, 'Gazza' gathered the ball in his own half and set off on a run, dismissing challenge after Aberdeen challenge, before steering a wonderful left-foot shot past Michael Watt. 'Eight-in-a-Row' had become reality. It came as little surprise when he scooped both 'Player of the Year' awards.

Although, the following year, his name seemed to appear as much on the front pages, there was still much to admire and write about in a footballing sense. Indeed, it was flashes of his genius that decided the ultimate destination of November's League Cup, when Rangers met Hearts in the final. In the second-half, the 'Jambos' had drawn level, cancelling out an earlier 'double' by Ally McCoist. Step forward Paul Gascoigne, to conjure up two sublime moments of magic and Rangers were virtually home and dry - despite the elements.

Against the same team, one month later, the Englishman ran the show in the 'Light Blues' emphatic 4-1 Tynecastle victory. Although it was really the year of Brian Laudrup, Paul, too, had played his part and was there at Tannadice on 7 May 1997 for the ultimate triumph. The player never completed another full season with the club, making just fourteen league appearances and scoring only three goals in 1997/98. It would certainly have been more but for a lengthy suspension after his 'red card' against Celtic in November. He joined Middlesbrough in March 1998 for approximately £3.5 million.

At the end of the day, Paul Gascoigne's contribution to two Championships in three seasons will not be forgotten by the masses that idolised him during his all-too-brief time in Scotland.

Rangers Career Statistics
Games: 103 Goals: 39 League Championship Medals: 2
Scottish Cup Medals: 1 League Cup Medals: 1

McEWAN'S
LAGER

RONNIE McKINNON

t was not all joy and light that November night in Lisbon, when Rangers progressed to the quarter-final stage of the European Cup Winners' Cup tournament. Naturally, the team were not to know that glory beckoned the following May in Barcelona but the players did realise, cruel and sad as it was, their centre-half would play no further part in the competition. Ronnie McKinnon's leg was broken in two places and his season was over.

To this day, the half-back line of 'Greig, McKinnon and Baxter,' from that great side of the early sixties, is still revered by all friends of Rangers. Following his arrival at Ibrox in 1959 (from the 'Juniors'), a spell in the reserve side saw the 'half-back' begin his evolvement into a centre-half and by the latter part of Season 1961/62, the No.5 jersey was his. Some months later, McKinnon was criticised when Tottenham Hotspur crushed the 'Light Blues' in the Cup Winners' Cup, his aerial ability being brought into question following the 5-2 defeat at White Hart Lane in late October 1962. Manager Scot Symon's faith was justified, however, as Rangers lifted the League and Scottish Cup 'double' in the early summer of 1963.

One year on, a marvellous domestic 'treble' adorned the Trophy Room and McKinnon, with Greig and Baxter beside him, now oozed style and class. Another Scottish Cup (in 1965/66) and two League Cups (in 1964/65 and 1970/71, as captain, deputising for the injured Greig) would complete his Ibrox collection, along with the twenty-eight Scotland 'Caps' won at international level. It is also worth noting that, when Celtic were firing on all cylinders during the latter years of the sixties, it was primarily the combination of Greig and McKinnon who held the team together. The centre-half was 'freed' by Rangers at the end of Season 1972/73 and left for Durban and South Africa.

The cruel twist of fate that denied the player glory on a hot Spanish night was a sickening blow but, at least, McKinnon did receive his own European Cup Winners' Cup medal in the days that followed the game. Manager Jock Wallace saw to that. It was a highly appropriate gesture to a truly magnificent club servant.

Rangers Career Statistics
Games: 473 Goals: 3 League Championship Medals: 2
Scottish Cup Medals: 4 League Cup Medals: 3
European Medals: 1

ANDY GORAM

In many ways it was just typical of the man. It would be extremely difficult to name any other player who could miss six Premier and 'Champions League' encounters through injury and then return (without being 100% fit) to play a true hero's role in a highly significant victory. But then again, Andrew Lewis Goram was no ordinary mortal.

As they awaited kick-off on 14 November 1996, the Rangers faithful gathered at Parkhead breathed a collective sigh of relief on hearing the announcement that 'The Goalie' was back. They knew deep inside that Scotland's No.1 would be needed that night. So it was to prove, as he produced a whole string of impressive stops that, yet again, broke the heart of Celtic. A magnificent comeback was capped with a superb penalty save from Van Hooijdonk late on, as the home side pressed to equalise Brian Laudrup's early goal. The Scot or the Dane? It was a toss-up for 'Man of the Match'. Goram was now back for good, or so it was thought, until further injury came calling in March 1997, as Rangers made their final push towards the glory that would be 'Nine-in-a-Row'.

For the majority of Ibrox 'Bears', there was a feeling of sadness that Andy was missing on that great day at Tannadice in May. Few deserved to be there more than him. As celebrations ensued in the days that followed, the season's highlights were naturally re-lived over and over again. Many would comment on the significance of that penalty save back in November, which ultimately took Rangers three points ahead of their closest rivals. Some would even suggest that it was the moment that ended Celtic's championship challenge for the season - but that was open to debate. Nobody would deny, however, that it was supremely important in the grand scheme of things. And for that alone, Andy Goram deserves the accolades.

During the previous season of 1995/96, Rangers had met Celtic on six occasions (winning three and drawing the others) without feeling the pain of defeat. To remain unbeaten against their greatest rivals all year owed a great debt, once again, to the remarkable dependability of the man 'between the sticks'. To cite but two examples:
a) In the traditional 'Ne'erday' encounter, the game was evenly balanced at 0-0, when Celtic midfielder, Phil O'Donnell, struck a blistering left-foot shot on the run from just outside the box. Goram's fingertips pushed the ball onto the post and Richard Gough cleared.
b) The previous November, the fans had witnessed a fabulous 3-3 draw at Ibrox. Certainly one of the main talking points that day was Andy's quite miraculous stop from a point-blank Van Hooijdonk volley, with the Rangers defence posted missing. Even now, it's still difficult to believe the quality of that save to deny the Dutchman.

It was Walter Smith, at the beginning of his first 'full' season in charge at Ibrox, that brought the player to the club, with £1 million transferring east to the Hibernian bank account. Before long, it became apparent to the 'Follow-Followers' that Andy Goram was a class apart - a 'keeper without equal.

And that's really how it stayed for seven wonderful years, until the end of that particular era in the summer of 1998, when more than one Ibrox legend left Govan behind for the very last time. Someone said of 'The Goalie' that it would be possible to count on the fingers of one hand, the mistakes he would make in a season. Reviewing any of his years with the club, even that ridiculously low figure is difficult to reach.

It was always Goram's goal to be the best. He was.

Rangers Career Statistics
Games: 258 Goals: Nil League Championship Medals: 5
Scottish Cup Medals: 3 League Cup Medals: 2

adidas

ALEX MacDONALD

Imagine the dream sequence: Rangers are your boyhood heroes and all you ever want to do is play for them. It happens. Then, in a major game against Celtic - a Cup Final, for example - you score the winning goal. It happens. Waking up, you realise that it could never occur in the real world........or could it?

Manager, Davie White, paid St. Johnstone £50,000 for the services of twenty-year-old Alex MacDonald in November 1968. It took some time for the player to be accepted but after a period of time, the Ibrox legions and the competitive midfielder were in harmony. His, passionate commitment, to the Rangers cause ensured folk hero status down Govan way, as 'Doddie' became one of them.

Alex scored many crucial goals for the team, none more so than on that dangerous road to Barcelona and Cup Winners' Cup glory in 1972. In the first round, following a 1-1 draw against French outfit, Rennes, in Brittany, he netted the only goal of the game at Ibrox, late in the first-half. Six months later, in the quarter-final (second leg), the Italians of Torino arrived in Glasgow on the back of another 1-1 draw. But again the outcome was the just the same - a solitary MacDonald strike took Rangers through.

'Doddie' was an integral part of Jock Wallace's 'treble'-winning sides of Seasons 1975/76 and 1977/78. A total of three Championships, four Scottish Cups and four League Cups were won by the player on the domestic front and, of course, further afield in Spain, a European Cup Winners' Cup Medal. He proudly wore the blue over 500 times, scoring 94 goals in the process. The midfielder joined Hearts in 1980 and then became player-manager of the Gorgie club, taking them close to an historic Scottish League and Cup double. With the Edinburgh side, he was named 'Manager of the Year' in 1986. It was, however, much earlier (in 1975) that a certain boyhood dream became reality.......

In the October of that year, Rangers met Celtic in the final of the League Cup. The game was evenly balanced before a flying, second-half header ignited the blue touchpaper at one end of Hampden and decided the trophy's ultimate destination.

One goal and one man, Alex MacDonald.

Rangers Career Statistics
Games : 503 Goals : 94 League Championship Medals : 3
Scottish Cup Medals : 4 League Cup Medals : 4
European Medals : 1

MARK HATELEY

For many of those with Rangers in their heart, it was the quote of the season. When asked, in March 1997, how it felt to be coming back to Ibrox after his spell in England with Queen's Park Rangers, the big man simply replied: 'Coming back? No, I'm coming home!'

Yet, it is common knowledge that Mark Hateley did not exactly receive the warmest of welcomes when he first wore the blue of Rangers at the start of Season 1990/91. In fact, a minority of so-called supporters were downright hostile to the striker, who had spent most of the previous year (at Monaco) trying to shake off a troublesome ankle injury and was, obviously, far from 100% fit. Just imagine, though, questioning the ability of someone who had spent three years with AC Milan, won 32 England 'Caps' and played regularly at the very highest level.

Those initial shouts of abuse would return to haunt them, however, when Mark's two goals against Aberdeen at Ibrox delivered the Championship in early May. His first strike that day (a fifteen-yard header after soaring like an avenging angel above the red defence)) is now the very stuff of legend.

Hateley's next campaign began with a 'hat-trick' against St. Johnstone (6-0, 10.8.91) and then, more famously, on a rare hot late-August afternoon, the striker claimed both Rangers goals at Parkhead in the 2-0 victory. This period also ended on a high, with the player scoring Ranger's first in the Scottish Cup Final against Airdrie (2-1, 9.5.92), when the trophy returned to the Ibrox Trophy Room for the first time since 1981.

In Season 1992/93, he provided a seemingly endless list of highlights..........the magnificent left-foot volley from 25 yards at Elland Road against Leeds in the European Cup, the ball nestling in the back of the net even before 'keeper Lukic had returned to earth.....the inch-perfect curling cross for Ally's diving header and goal No. 2 in the same game.....Mark's own headed equaliser against Marseille that almost took the roof off Ibrox......the burst of pace, superb run and sweet, low shot from an acute angle, for Ranger's second and decisive Scottish Cup Final goal. Who was it questioned his ability?

'Attila' was now the most feared striker in football north of the border. He was voted 'Player of the Year' by the Scottish Football Writers' Association at the end of Season 1993/94, thus becoming the first Englishman to win this prestigious award. Unfortunately, injury played a major part in his last year with the club and at the beginning of Season 1995/96, Mark joined the Rangers of London, then bossed by former colleague, Ray Wilkins. That was not quite the end of the story, however, as the 'Hit-Man' did return, briefly, to help the cause, prior to the 'Nine-in-a-Row' decider at Parkhead.

To the tune of England's soccer anthem for the 1996 European Championships, 'Football's Coming Home', the 'Bears' greeted his arrival on the park for that Celtic match with, 'Hateley's Coming Home'. Even though the player only lasted some 66 minutes, he undoubtedly played his part in a momentous Rangers victory. To say that the Celtic defence had no answers to the questions he posed them, leading the line in his own inimitable style, is an understatement.

No greater compliment can be paid.

Rangers Career Statistics
Games: 222 Goals: 115 League Championship Medals: 5
Scottish Cup Medals: 2 League Cup Medals: 3

McEWAN'S
Mitre

JOHN GREIG

ere, there and everywhere, it came as no major surprise when John Greig was recently voted 'Greatest Ever Ranger', since the man is a true Ibrox legend. More than any other post-war player, he embodied the true spirit of the club. A natural leader, with a staggering 755 appearances in the blue to his credit, John's first game was against Airdrie in the League Cup of September 1961. A few days short of his nineteenth birthday, he scored on his debut after only ten minutes.

Greig won the first of his five Championship medals in 1963. By then, any Glaswegian schoolboy could recite the Rangers half-back line of 'Greig, McKinnon and Baxter' easier than a line of French! The following season, it was the domestic 'treble', a notable feat also achieved much later in both 1975/76 and 1977/78, when the defender was still an integral part of the 'Light Blue' rearguard.

When Celtic reigned supreme in Scotland and were winning their own version of 'Nine-in-a-Row', in many ways it was John who, as a truly inspiring Club Captain, held the team together. Even though injured, he was rightly present at Easter Road in April 1975 when the Championship was regained after that long, barren period in the shadows. Appearing on the park for the last few minutes, he was given the true hero's welcome he so richly deserved.

Probably the abiding image of John Greig is with the European Cup Winners' Cup on a lap of honour at Ibrox (his beard was soon to disappear!) after that glorious Barcelona night in May 1972. Indeed, he had been part of the Rangers team that lost to Bayern Munich in the final of the same competition five years earlier.

The player wore the dark blue of Scotland a total of forty-four times, playing twenty-one games in succession. In November 1965, his famous solo goal defeated Italy 1-0 in a World Cup qualifying match at Hampden. For nearly three years, Greig was also captain of his country. Following the shock resignation of Jock Wallace in late May 1978, it was a case of club captain one day, manager the next. Both the Scottish and League Cups were won twice during his five years in the hot seat but the Championship was never realised and on 28 October 1983, he resigned.

As a player and captain of Rangers, John Greig stands tall with the very best. There can be no higher praise.

Rangers Career Statistics

Games: 755 Goals: 120 League Championship Medals: 5

Scottish Cup Medals: 6 League Cup Medals: 4

European Medals: 1

RICHARD GOUGH

On the afternoon of Sunday 16 March 1997, Celtic were presented with one final chance to stop Rangers' ultimate goal of equalling their own jealously guarded record of the 1960s and 1970s. It was judgement day in the quest for 'Nine-in-a-Row'. Most neutrals were tipping a Celtic victory in the wake of their Scottish Cup triumph over Rangers (2-0) some ten days earlier and the Ibrox club's subsequent 'home' defeat by Dundee United. Central defender, Richard Gough, had missed both these games through injury but now he was back. Leading by example, he played a true captain's role and the rest, as they say, is history.

Rangers finally got their man in October 1987, when Graeme Souness paid Tottenham Hotspur a record fee of £1 million for the player's services. The club had, indeed, tried to sign Gough previously, when he was with Dundee United, but the Taysiders refused to allow a transfer. His second game (and first goal) in blue was the contentious 2-2 draw with Celtic at Ibrox, when three players were sent off. Richard's last-minute equaliser for nine-man 'Gers is already the stuff of legend. By the following season's end, Rangers were Champions once again and that incredible sequence had begun. Eight more magical years would also include 'trebles' in both 1992 and 1993, with Gough as inspirational as ever.

Inheriting the armband from a departing Terry Butcher in the autumn of 1990, the player was proudly lifting silverware within a matter of weeks, when his extra-time goal clinched the 2-1 League Cup Final win over Celtic. Richard Gough would go on to become the club's most successful captain since Davie Meiklejohn, who guided the 'Light Blues' to twelve league titles back in the twenties and thirties.

After Rangers had secured their eighth successive Championship (with closest rivals, Celtic, only losing once all season), manager Walter Smith suggested that, had it not been for missing several fixtures through injury in the February/March period, Richard could well have been voted 'Player of the Year' 1995/96. Certainly his form that season had been quite awe-inspiring, as the 'Light Blues' faced up to the challenge of a born-again Celtic from across the city.

Needless to say, the hopes and dreams of all fans lay in Season 1996/97. Gough's return to that Rangers rearguard before the vital Parkhead league encounter in March proved crucial and some five weeks later at Tannadice, the dream was finally realised. There was no one prouder, or more emotional, as he held aloft the Championship trophy that April evening. He had been there way back in Season 1988/89 when it all began.

Richard Gough - A Man For All Seasons.

Rangers Career Statistics
Games: 427 Goals: 34 League Championship Medals: 9
Scottish Cup Medals: 3 League Cup Medals: 6

adidas

WILLIE JOHNSTON

ometimes a player's career is so clouded in controversy that it is difficult to look beyond the negative. Take the case of Willie Johnston, for example, with his unenviable record of sendings-off and infamous early homecoming from the 1978 Scotland World Cup squad in Argentina. Look beyond that, to his time at Ibrox in particular and see, instead, a hugely talented left-winger who played a leading role in Rangers' finest hour on foreign soil.

Signed from Lochore Welfare Juniors in Fife, 'Bud' made his Rangers debut against St. Johnstone in the League Cup game of 29 August, 1964. He was extremely fast, with amazing dribbling skills and an acute eye for goal. By the end of the following season, the winger had played in forty-eight league and cup games (scoring thirteen goals) and gained what was to be his only Scottish Cup medal, when Celtic were beaten by Kai Johansen's wonder goal.

Few Rangers fans need reminding of Johnston's major contribution when the club so famously triumphed in Europe. In the opening game (against Rennes in Brittany) and the quarter-final, first-leg (versus Torino in Italy) of the 1971/72 Cup Winners' Cup, it was the winger who struck for the Ibrox club on each occasion to secure 1-1 draws, thus ensuring priceless 'away' goals prior to the return encounters in Glasgow. Even though Colin Stein opened the scoring when Rangers met Moscow Dynamo in the May final, it was a double from Johnston (one each side of the interval) that decided the trophy's ultimate destination. Due reward for the player who collected a losers' medal after the Bayern Munich final of 1967.

By December 1972, Willie was on his way to West Bromwich Albion, where he was also a success. Indeed, it was during this period in England that he travelled as part of the Scotland squad to Argentina and the 1978 World Cup. Following the disastrous defeat by Peru, he failed a drug test and returned home, his Scotland career over after twenty-two 'Caps'. Johnston actually returned to Ibrox in August 1980 for two seasons, when John Greig was manager, before moving on again.

Despite all the debate that surrounded his years in football, Willie Johnston will always be remembered down Govan way. Especially for the most wonderful of nights in Barcelona.

Rangers Career Statistics
Games : 393 Goals : 125
Scottish Cup Medals : 1 League Cup Medals : 2
European Medals : 1

BRIAN LAUDRUP

Only a select few truly capture the hearts and minds. Not many would dispute that Brian Laudrup was not only the most talented footballer to wear the blue of Rangers in modern times but also a perfect ambassador for the club. In his own way, a peerless prince.

Right from the beginning, it was obvious that here was a special talent. In his very first game for the club, against Motherwell at Ibrox on the opening day of Season 1994/95, the standard was set. A magnificent mazy run from just outside the Rangers penalty area left defenders trailing in his wake, as the Dane set up Duncan Ferguson's late winner in the 2-1 victory. Even at this stage, the £2.25 million paid to Fiorentina seemed quite a bargain.

The highlights increased as the year progressed. Indeed, his strike against Celtic at Hampden in the league race (3-1, 30.10.94) was a contender for goal of the campaign. The following season there was no dubiety, however and the award was his. It came in the Scottish Cup semi-final with old friends, Celtic, when, in sixty-seven minutes, Laudrup completed a majestic, flowing movement, involving Durie and Gascoigne, by lobbing the advancing Gordon Marshall from outside the penalty area to score.

As magical as this game was, it was nothing but a prelude compared to the final itself. The player produced a masterly display in the 5-1 demolition of Hearts, netting twice and creating all three others for Gordon Durie. That 1996 Scottish Cup Final will always be remembered as, 'The Day of Brian Laudrup'.

The year of 'Nine-in-a-Row' was, in many ways, also the year of the Dane. He was the controlling maestro behind Rangers' two best performances of the season, at Tynecastle and Pittodrie in December, when both Hearts (3-0) and Aberdeen (4-1) were swept aside. Of greater significance, was the fact that Celtic tasted defeat in four out of five league encounters, with Brian claiming both goals in the 1-0 triumphs of November and March. The latter spring clash virtually ended Celtic's faint hope of stopping Rangers relentless' pursuit of nine consecutive titles.

In May 1997, for the second time in three years, Laudrup was named 'Player of the Year' by the Scottish Football Writers' Association. Although his last season at Ibrox, before heading south for a very brief stay with Chelsea in London, was not successful, it was still a case of 'Thanks for the Memories'. His place in Ibrox legend was more than assured.

Brian Laudrup, a player touched by genius.

Rangers Career Statistics
Games: 150 Goals: 44 League Championship Medals: 3
Scottish Cup Medals: 1 League Cup Medals: 1

McEWANS
LAGER

TOMMY MacLEAN

For some forty years, beginning in the post-war era, Rangers were more than just a little fortunate when it came to the No.7 jersey. Quite simply, in each of those four decades, a quartet of blue legends filled that right-wing position - Waddell, Scott, Henderson and last but by no means least, Tommy McLean.

Willie Waddell brought the Kilmarnock player to Ibrox in 1971 for £65,000. McLean was, by this time, in his mid twenties and had already played for Scotland five times during his time down the coast in Ayrshire. In fact, it was Waddell who had taken the youngster to 'Killie' when he was manager there. 'Wee Tam' was an altogether different type of winger than his lauded predecessors, for his forte was pin-point accuracy with a football, whether it be a pass or a cross. Both the 'Derek' centre-forwards, Johnstone and Parlane, converted chances by the proverbial barrowload that were created by him.

By the end of his first season with Rangers, he had collected a European Cup Winners' Cup medal after the triumph in Barcelona. The following year in the Scottish Cup, his 'double' against Hibernian at Easter Road (in a replay) sent the Ibrox men through to the quarter-final. They would soon face old friends, Celtic, in the famous Centenary Final of 1973 and lift the trophy on a 3-2 scoreline.

In the winger's first Championship season at the club (1974/75), he was joint second top scorer with Derek Johnstone on fourteen goals. Only striker, Derek Parlane, surpassed that, with a total of seventeen strikes. Celebrations were even heartier twelve months down the line, when a domestic 'treble' was in the bag. Two years later, the feat was repeated and manager Jock Wallace was in the history books as the first Rangers manager to guide the club to two such 'trebles'.

McLean's last trophies with Rangers were both Cups, Scottish and League, in 1978/79. Following the defeat by Aberdeen in the Scottish Cup Final of May 1983, the player retired and became assistant to manager, John Greig, at Ibrox. He then worked with Jock Wallace (during his second spell in charge of the 'Light Blues') before going on to manage Morton, Motherwell (and a Scottish Cup win in 1991 for the Lanarkshire side), Hearts and Dundee United.

Any player would be honoured to stand comparison with the likes of Willie Waddell, Alex Scott and Willie Henderson. Indeed, in the eyes of many, Tommy McLean was the best of them all.

Rangers Career Statistics
Games: 452   Goals: 57   League Championship Medals: 3
Scottish Cup Medals: 4   League Cup Medals: 3
European Medals: 1

MAURICE JOHNSTON

In the early summer of 1989, there had been ample press and TV coverage regarding the fact that Maurice Johnston was to return to Celtic after his successful time in France with Nantes. Indeed, it was something of a coup for the club. Imagine the consternation, therefore, when, on 10th July, the striker was introduced to the awaiting media by Graeme Souness as Rangers' latest acquisition at £1.5 million. Certainly, many season ticket holders were not happy with the signing of this high profile ex-Celt and Roman Catholic but to others, it was a case of, 'let's wait and see'. The wait would not be long.

History was in the making on a cold November's day when the 'Old Firm' met at Ibrox on league duty. The Rangers supporters knew that, sooner or later, Mo would score against his old club. The player knew it, too – it was inevitable. But few could have envisaged that it would happen in such dramatic and winning fashion.

Near the end, with the score still 0-0 and stalemate close on the horizon, Johnston made his move. Hovering just outside the enemy box, he controlled a loose ball before hitting a sweet, low, right-foot shot that nestled comfortably in the Celtic net. The look of total joy on Mo's face said it all, as he ran, socks round his ankles as per usual, to the Rangers faithful behind Bonner's goal to acknowledge their acclaim. Like Vesuvius, Ibrox had erupted. Although these extended celebrations earned him his first caution of the campaign, the victory and the day were his. Many would say that the 1989/90 Season was his as well.

It was not the hard-working striker's first goal for his new club. That had come at Ibrox in early September, when Aberdeen were beaten 1-0. Three weeks later, Hearts suffered the same fate with Johnston again netting the solitary strike. By season's end, with a tally of fifteen goals in the league, Johnston had, without a doubt, made his mark.That year, his partnership with Ally McCoist realised a total of thirty-five in all domestic competitions. The Championship was Govan bound once again.

Up front, Mo's next main partner was Mark Hateley (in Season 1990/91), with the duo netting twenty-one strikes between them in the battle with Aberdeen for the title. Although Hateley's name was covered in glory on that hot May day, Johnston, too, had played his part. Not only with an 'assist' for the second goal ('keeper Watt had failed to hold his initial shot thus allowing the 'Big Man' to convert the rebound) but also by his tireless running, as he covered each and every inch of the park in pursuit of the Championship.

On international duty with Scotland, the player gained a total of 38 'Caps'. In a fine 2-1 win over Sweden during 'Italia 90' (the 1990 World Cup Finals in Italy), Maurice scored from the penalty spot after he had been fouled. Earlier, in the qualifying stages, he struck both goals when France were beaten at Hampden. After winning two consecutive league titles at Ibrox, the player moved on to Everton for £1.75 million. Later in his career, both Hearts and Falkirk would benefit from his experience.

Certainly, no friend of Rangers will ever forget the events of that winter's day in 1989, when the inevitable became reality; but Johnston contributed much more to the cause than just goals during his spell in the blue. It is not an overstatement to say that he played for the jersey as if to the manor born.

Rangers Career Statistics
Games: 100 Goals: 46
League Championship Medals: 2

McEWAN'S
LAGER

WILLIE WADDELL

Who was the greatest of them all? An almost impossible question to answer, as opinions will most surely differ. One thing is certain, though and there can be little debate - in the long history of Rangers Football Club, no single person has done or achieved more than Willie Waddell.

As a player, it all began with a sensational first-team appearance at the ripe old age of seventeen. Not only did Waddell 'roast' his opposite number but he also scored the only goal of the game in this pre-season 'friendly' against Arsenal at Ibrox in 1938. Not for the last time would a defender welcome the sound of the final whistle and the sight of that No.7 jersey disappearing up the tunnel!

In time, he would become an integral part of the great post-war Rangers side that dominated Scottish football in the late forties and early fifties. Centre-forward, Willie Thornton, benefited more than most, by converting on numerous occasions, the winger's deadly accurate crosses. In fact, a high percentage of the striker's goals were scored with the head. But Waddell, a pacey and powerful man himself, was also a seasoned finisher, as his 56 goals testify. The pair were, indeed, a quite lethal duo.

League Championships followed in 1946/47, 1948/49 and 1952/53, with the Scottish Cup also returning to Ibrox in1948/89 and1952/53. In that 'double' season of 1952/53, it was Waddell who scored the equaliser on the last day of the league campaign at Queen of the South, securing the title on goal difference from Hibernian. Having won 17 International 'Caps' as well, Willie Waddell then retired as a player in the summer of 1956.

As manager of Kilmarnock, he famously took the Ayrshire team to the Championship in 1965 before returning to Rangers in the same capacity, after the sacking of Davie White in November1969. Some two and a half years later, Waddell would guide his team to Barcelona and watch their greatest ever triumph unfold in the Nou Camp Stadium on the 24th of May 1972. Weeks later, coach Jock Wallace was appointed manager, with Mr. Waddell becoming general manager.

On the stadium front, the 'New Ibrox' was instigated by his vision in the wake of the disaster of 1971, when sixty-six people were tragically killed. Willie Waddell would see this dream of re-birth come true.

Before passing away in 1992, he had served his beloved Rangers in several capacities, including player, manager, general manager, managing director and vice-chairman. Willie Waddell was unique.

Rangers Career Statistics

Games: 296 Goals: 56 League Championship Medals: 4
Scottish Cup Medals: 2

RAY WILKINS

His stay in Glasgow lasted a mere two years, yet the name Ray Wilkins is still held in awe down Ibrox way. Considered the finest midfield talent to don the blue since the genius that was Jim Baxter, 'Butch' joined Rangers in November 1987 after a short, disappointing stay in Paris with Saint Germain.

Sporting a footballing pedigree second to none, the Englishman had worn the colours of Chelsea, Manchester United and AC Milan, as well as playing for his country no less than 84 times. During his time in Manchester, the 'Reds' lifted the FA Cup in both 1982 and 1983.

After Wilkins' debut in the 3-2 victory over Hearts (Ibrox, 28.11.87), he remained an ever-present in the team for the rest of that season, even notching a solitary goal against St. Mirren in February when Rangers won 4-0. The player endeared himself to 'Bears' everywhere by always ushering celebrating players towards the crowd - he knew the true importance of the Ibrox legions. The first of his three Scottish medals was acquired this first year, when Aberdeen were victims on League Cup Final day.

Season 1988/89 had hardly begun before reigning Champions, Celtic, came calling on a gloriously hot, late-August afternoon. Very soon Ray Wilkins would score what was to be his only league goal of the campaign. . . very soon Ray Wilkins would be a Ranger for life. Ten minutes before the interval, with the game evenly balanced at 1-1, a clearance header by Paul McStay dropped just outside the area. Lurking like a predator, Wilkins pounced and hit the most perfectly judged and flighted right-foot volley, which screamed past 'keeper Andrews. He could do nothing but spectate with grudging admiration! Rangers were ahead and would not be caught. A famous 5-1 victory was unfolding.

In due course, with 'Razor's' assistance, the Championship returned to Ibrox that year along with the League Cup, which was retained. A 'treble' was on the cards by late May but 'Lady Luck' dealt a black hand. Both Ray and fellow midfielder, Ian Ferguson, were to miss the Scottish Cup Final through injury, thus opening the door of advantage to opponents, Celtic, who won 1-0.

Wilkins was an ever-present in the league the following year until his last game for Rangers, against Dunfermline at Ibrox on 25 November, 1989. He had decided to return home to London for family reasons. Even allowing for the grey of the weather, an air of depression hung over the stadium. A standing ovation for the player from 40,000 people, as he stood alone in the centre-circle at 4.45 pm, echoed throughout Govan. Certainly, this helped dispense the gloom but knowing that he would never wear the blue of Rangers again, Ray Wilkins was not the only one to shed a tear.

Rangers Career Statistics

Games: 96 Goals: 3 League Championship Medals: 2
League Cup Medals: 1

McEWAN'S
LAGER

WILLIE THORNTON

illie Thornton, the player, was an 'old fashioned' centre-forward, not only in the way he played the game but also in his unparalleled sportsmanship. He had style, guile, skill in abundance and the priceless knack of scoring goals, particularly with his head. In this respect, the partnership with his legendary right-wing team-mate and great friend, Willie Waddell, was devastating.Thornton was the first post-war Ranger to break the 100 goal barrier and Waddell's pinpoint crosses ensured that a high proportion of those goals were headed.

Willie joined Rangers from Winchburgh Albion in March, 1936, at the tender age of sixteen. Salary: £1 a week! His first-team debut was against Partick Thistle at Firhill on 2 January 1937, when his appearance (at outside-right) made him one of the youngest-ever Rangers. Following twenty outings in Season 1937/38, the player established himself as a regular the following year, which brought the first of his four League Championship medals.

Like many of his generation, Willie 'lost' the best part of six years to the Second World War, during which he served with distinction in the Duke of Atholl's Scottish Horse, to this day the only private regiment in the British Army. He was decorated with the Military Medal for his gallantry in the Sicilian campaign.

International duty beckoned for the first time in 1946, when Thornton wore the dark blue against Switzerland on 15 May, at Hampden. Scotland won 3-1. Later that summer, against England at Maine Road, he claimed both goals in the 2-2 draw. Surprisingly, the striker appeared for his country in only seven full international games.

In Season 1947/48, the post-war demand for football saw attendances soar. A staggering crowd of 143,570 (a British record) watched the Scottish Cup semi-final between Rangers and Hibernian, when a solitary Willie Thornton goal, from a Willie Waddell cross, decided the issue. Final opponents, Morton, were also beaten by a single headed goal– but this time the scorer was Billy Williamson, in extra time after a replay. Even greater glory enveloped the club the following year, when a domestic 'treble' of League Championship, Scottish Cup and League Cup was achieved by a team in Scotland for the very first time. The electric 'hit-man' scored thirty-six goals in all competitions, playing a major role in this unprecedented success.

The April Scottish Cup Final of 1950 was another memorable day. Willie was quite outstanding, as he netted twice in the 3-0 victory over East Fife and came so close to establishing a milestone for the club. A third strike had been disallowed (for offside), thus denying him the honour of becoming the first-ever Rangers player to score a 'hat-trick' in the final.

Voted 'Player of the Year' in 1952, Willie Thornton retired two years later in June1954. Management duties followed at Dundee and Partick Thistle, before returning to Ibrox as assistant manager, first to Davie White, then to his old partner, Willie Waddell. Interestingly, he actually had a brief spell as interim manager between White and Waddell, taking charge of the team for two winning matches - making him the only Rangers manager in history with a 100% record!

In time, he became custodian of the Ibrox Trophy Room and match-day host in the Thornton Suite. This true gentleman died in August 1991 at the age of 71. Much of the lifeblood of football is history and legend. In Willie Thornton, Rangers have a legend of the first order.

Rangers Career Statistics
Games: 303 Goals: 188 League Championship Medals: 4
Scottish Cup Medals: 3 League Cup Medals: 2

ALLY McCOIST

Not everybody is accorded a hero's welcome when they first wear the blue of Rangers. Surprising as it may seem, a certain Alistair McCoist fell into that category, for he was not always idolised by the masses down Govan way.

After signing for the club in June 1983 (having previously rejected their advances on, not one but two separate occasions) many 'Bears', understandably, questioned the player's Ibrox commitment. The striker worked hard to win over their support and the rest, as they say, is history.

Ally was top scorer for six consecutive seasons from 1983/84 to 1988/89, netting thirty-five, twenty-five, forty-one, forty-one, forty-nine and twenty-five goals respectively. On the last day of Season 1991/92, McCoist claimed not only his 200th Scottish League goal but also Rangers 100th of the campaign, at Pittodrie, when he scored twice and Aberdeen fell 2-0. Also that year, the prestigious European 'Golden Boot' trophy and Scottish 'Player of the Year' awards (from both the football writers and his fellow professionals) occupied positions side by side in the McCoist household. Twelve months later, he became the only player ever to retain the 'Golden Boot', with thirty-four goals converted in the same number of games.

Old friends, Celtic, suffered at his hand on more occasions than can be recalled but certainly his 'hat-tricks' in the Glasgow Cup Final of 1986 (3-2, 9.5.86) and the League Cup Final of 1984 (3-2, 25.3.84) are worth highlighting, as 'Super' became the first Ranger to net three against them in two encounters. And there was, of course, that night of the Glasgow monsoon in March 1992, when ten men in light blue defied both the elements and a Celtic onslaught to reach the Scottish Cup Final. Ally's name was on the game's solitary goal.

Two particular strikes feature high on most fans' list of McCoist favourites:
1) the diving header that finally silenced both Elland Road and the English media when Leeds were beaten 2-1 in the European Cup of November 1992.
2) the audacious overhead kick and subsequent winner, after appearing as substitute against Hibernian, in the League Cup Final of October 1993.

A bad leg break playing for Scotland in Portugal in 1993 put Ally out of the game for some time but – in due course, he was back for club and country and ended Season 1995/96 with twenty goals to his credit. The McCoist time at Ibrox ended with the beginning of the Advocaat era. Even in his last season with the club (1997/98), it was the player's attitude that lifted the team late on for one final push towards a possible 'double' – but it was not to be, despite all his valiant efforts.

Strikers with Ally McCoist's predatory instincts are a rare breed. Many, many thousands will be forever thankful that he was a Ranger.

Rangers Career Statistics
Games: 581 Goals: 355 League Championship Medals: 8
Scottish Cup Medals: 1 League Cup Medals: 9

adidas
McEWAN'S
LAGER

GEORGE YOUNG

In the words of the song, he was a 'big, big man'........in every sense. Six feet, two inches in height and fifteen stones in weight, this power-house Rangers icon was captain of the great Ibrox post-war side that dominated Scottish football in the late 1940s and early 1950s.

Born of Grangemouth stock in 1922, George Young signed professional terms with the club in 1941 and following the end of the Second World War, took his place at the heart of that blue line that would soon become renowned throughout the country as the famous 'Iron Curtain' defence. A rearguard that, in six full seasons of 180 league games, lost only 180 goals.

A superb tackler, 'Corky' (he always carried a champagne cork for luck), could also hit uncannily accurate 50 to 60 yard passes, turning defence into attack in an instant. With forward players of the calibre of Messrs Thornton and Waddell, this distinct advantage was a regular and successful Rangers ploy. At the time, the team were often unfairly tagged as 'route one' specialists - the Wimbledon of their day! Although more of an obvious centre-half, due to the presence of the masterly Willie Woodburn in the side, most of Young's appearances were in the right-back position. He did reclaim that central role, however, after Woodburn's 'sine die' suspension in September 1954.

In the Scottish Cup Final of April 1949, Geordie scored twice (with two penalties) in the 4-1 win over opponents, Clyde, when Rangers achieved Scottish football's first-ever domestic 'treble'. Four years on, even more of a captain's part was required against Aberdeen in the Final of 1953, when goalkeeper, George Niven, was stretchered off in the first period. 'Corky' filled the gap 'between the sticks' for some eighteen minutes before Niven returned, swathed in bandages, at the start of the second-half. The game finished all square at 1-1, with the 'Light Blues' lifting the trophy after a 1-0 replay victory. Incidentally, a crowd of some 129,760 watched the first game, followed by a 113,700 attendance for the second.

His Ibrox record of six League Championships, four Scottish Cups and two League Cups speaks for itself. Certainly no less impressive is the Scotland connection, having played for his country 53 times (with 34 of those appearances being consecutive) and captaining the 'Dark Blues' a record 48 times. He wore the national colours for the last time when Switzerland were beaten 2-1 in Basle. Aged 34, George Young retired in 1957 but later managed Third Lanark for a three year period.

A great club captain and a Rangers giant, in many more ways than one.

Rangers Career Statistics
Games: 428 Goals: 31 League Championship Medals: 6
Scottish Cup Medals: 4 League Cup Medals: 2

STUART McCALL

Stuart McCall travelled from Merseyside to Govan in the summer of 1991 and almost immediately, became an indispensable part of the Rangers midfield. His tenacious, battling qualities encouraged manager, Walter Smith, to bring the fiery Scot north (for a fee of £1.2 million) in the days when teams could only play three 'foreigners' (maximum) in any European competition.

Some players develop an affinity with a club's supporters almost immediately. Others never quite seem to break down that invisible barrier. Stu' rapidly joined the former category, the Ibrox legions realising from the outset that here, indeed, was a man who would play for the jersey until he dropped. He never gave less than everything, in season after season of inspirational performances.

His first goal for Rangers was against Sparta Prague in the European Champions' Cup, when he netted twice in the 2-1 October victory. By season's end, McCall had collected the first of his five League Championship medals with the club. In October 1992, he struck the first goal against Aberdeen in the Skol Cup Final, as Rangers triumphed 2-1. The following month at Parkhead, he slotted effortlessly into the right-back position as the 'Light Blues' progressed towards the domestic 'treble' following the 1-0 league victory. The record-breaking Rangers squad of Season 1992/93 was imbued throughout with tremendous spirit. As much as anyone, that never-say-die attitude was typified by Stuart McCall.

Week after week in 1994/95, the team had to be changed around, mainly due to an unbelievable run of injuries to key personnel. By early March and the latter stages of the push for '7th Heaven', he had become the season's only ever-present in terms of first-team appearances. At the start of the following season, Stuart's winning goal against Kilmarnock at Ibrox ensured a successful beginning to another long campaign. Most memorable was his tigerish 'Man of the Match' display in the Scottish Cup semi-final duel with Celtic in April, when he wore the captain's armband, deputising for the injured Richard Gough. He covered every blade of Hampden grass that day, driving Rangers on to another memorable triumph.

It somehow seemed inevitable that McCall would leave the club at the end of the 'Smith' era. He returned to his first club, Bradford (and the English Premiership for Season 1999/2000) but remains, at heart, a Rangers man.

Suffice to say that his inspirational midfield qualities are sorely missed.

Rangers Career Statistics
Games: 264 Goals: 20 League Championship Medals: 5
Scottish Cup Medals: 3 League Cup Medals: 2

McEWAN'S

DAVIE MEIKLEJOHN

t is a scenario that few players would openly relish. Try to imagine the pressure of the moment: Cup Final day at Hampden in April 1928 and a crowd of over 118,000 are holding their breath, awaiting a Rangers penalty-kick. Apart from the fact that the opponents are Cup-holders, Celtic and the score is still level at 0-0, Rangers have not won this particular trophy for all of twenty-five years. Surprisingly, it is neither of the regular 'spot-kick' specialists (McPhail or Cunningham) who step forward to place the ball. The man walking slowly into the area is Davie Meiklejohn.

The Govan born player arrived at Ibrox in 1919 from Maryhill Juniors, destined to become one of the all-time great Rangers players. In time, defender 'Meek' would be captain of the club and wear that most famous of jerseys 635 times, winning twelve Championships and five Scottish Cups in the process. He would also twice captain his country and win a total of fifteen 'Caps' in the dark blue of Scotland.

Since 1903, the Scottish Cup had proved an impossible lady to bed and indeed, there was much talk of a hoodoo surrounding the Govan team and this competition following their many years of failure. A close encounter was envisaged when Rangers lined up against Celtic on April 14 1928, Cup Final day. Despite almost constant Celtic pressure in the first-half, there was no scoring at the break, thanks mainly to superb rearguard work and a quite miraculous save by 'keeper, Tom Hamilton, from Paddy Connolly. Ten minutes into the second-half, a net-bound Fleming volley was fisted away by McStay, with Celtic goalkeeper, John Thomson, well beaten. Although the ball was well over the line, a penalty was awarded, as silence enshrouded the old stadium.

Deputising as captain for the injured Tommy Muirhead that day, Davie Meiklejohn decided the responsibility, awesome as it was, belonged to him and no one else. Totally focused, he struck a perfect penalty and Rangers were one-up. As a new-found confidence rapidly seeped through the team, Bob McPhail claimed a second thirteen minutes later, with Sandy Archibald making it three almost immediately after that. The rout was complete when winger Archibald made it 4-0 (with five minutes of play remaining) and one hoodoo was well and truly smashed.

With the party in full swing, many reflected on the game's turning point and that crucial moment in the history of Rangers Football Club, when Davie Meiklejohn stepped forward to place the ball and give birth to legend. Cometh the hour, cometh the man.

Rangers Career Statistics
Games : 635 Goals : 44 League Championship Medals : 12
Scottish Cup Medals : 5

GRAEME SOUNESS

ny Rangers victory over their greatest rivals is naturally cause for celebration. In this respect, January 1, 1987 at Ibrox was no different, as, on a miserable winter's day, thousands of blue revellers danced in the rain and snow toasting a 2-0 result. But something else happened that day and it was all to do with *the way* victory had been achieved - Graeme Souness strode the sodden turf like a Colossus, encouraging his team to play with an arrogance and confidence not seen for a very long time. Celtic were beaten in more ways than one and psychologically, suffered a huge blow.

Graeme James Souness was a world-class footballer, of that there is no doubt. His record with Liverpool (after joining from Middlesbrough for a record transfer between English clubs of £352,000 in January 1973) boasted three European Championships, five English Championships and four English League Cups. There was also the small matter of 54 Scotland 'Caps'! Following two seasons in Genoa with Serie 'A' club, Sampdoria, he arrived in Glasgow in the spring of 1986 to become the first-ever player-manager of Rangers. Scottish Football was about to change forever as the sleeping giant awoke.

He set about rebuilding and by the time Season 1986/87 kicked-off at Easter Road, both the England deputy-captain, Terry Butcher and the England No.2 goalkeeper, Chris Woods, were part of the line-up that would end a nine-year Championship famine at Pittodrie the following May. Souness' playing return to the country was not memorable, however, as he was sent-off in that first game in Edinburgh. If nothing else, however, it was apparent that, despite defeat, there had been a re-birth of team spirit in the Rangers squad. This team would not be easily pushed aside when the going got tough.

In his five years at Ibrox, the club won silverware every season, with four Championships and four League Cups adorning the Trophy Room. The Scottish Cup was the only major trophy not captured during his reign. There is little doubt, also, that it was because of the man himself that players of the calibre of Trevor Steven, Gary Stevens, Ray Wilkins and Richard Gough, plus the aforementioned Butcher and Woods, deemed to wear the blue. Friends of Rangers have much to be thankful for.

Controversy seemed to shadow much of his time in Scotland but it was the signing of ex-Celt, Maurice Johnston, that captured more headlines than anything else. Once the dust settled, Rangers' first high-profile Roman Catholic player would prove his worth, partnering both Ally McCoist and Mark Hateley in two Championship seasons, 1989/90 and 1990/91. It had been another Souness masterstroke.

Eventually, in April 1991, the lure of Liverpool proved too strong and he returned to Anfield as manager, leaving Rangers with four games still to play and a Championship still to be decided. Walter Smith was promoted to take charge and continue the club's development.

In time, Celtic's jealously guarded record of 'Nine-in-a-Row' would be equalled. Although the historic sequence actually started with the Championship secured at Ibrox against Hearts in the spring of 1989, in many ways the real beginning was on that cold 'Ne'erday' back in 1987, when Souness' team began to believe in the impossible.

His worth to Rangers, on and since that fateful day, should never be underestimated or forgotten.

Rangers Career Statistics
Games: 73 Goals: 5
League Championship Medals: 1

McEWAN'S
LAGER

ROBERT RUSSELL

The silky, lean midfielder, signed by Jock Wallace from Shettleston Juniors in 1977, was one of a select band of players that any true football supporter, regardless of their chosen colours, could admire and appreciate. He exuded class, with a capital 'C'.

A contemporary of Davie Cooper and Gordon Smith (both of whom arrived at Ibrox that same summer), Russell scored in Rangers' opening 'away' fixtures in the league campaign, a 3-1 defeat at Aberdeen and a 4-0 victory against Partick Thistle at Firhill. At the end of that season, Jock Wallace's team lifted a domestic 'treble' of Championship, Scottish Cup and League Cup, with the manager now having achieved this elusive feat in two of the previous three years.

Although twelve months later it was only (!) a 'double' of both cups, Russell himself had netted a rare 'hat-trick' at Ibrox earlier on league duty, when Hearts ventured west at the end of April. There are two more important games, however, that do stand out in an illustrious ten-year career of wearing the blue :
1) against PSV Eindhoven in the European Cup (1978). Following a marvellous 2-1 aggregate victory over Italian champions, Juventus (whose squad included no less than nine members of the national side), in the first round, Rangers were drawn against the Dutch. A no-scoring draw in Glasgow gave the 'Light Blues' little hope for the second leg in Holland, since the Eindhoven side were unbeaten at home in any European competition. It looked even bleaker when they netted in less than a minute's play! Rangers fought back and the score was tied at 2-2 with three minutes remaining. It was then that Bobby Russell made history when, running on to a Tommy McLean pass, he curled the ball round the advancing 'keeper into the net. It won the BBC award for 'Goal of the Year'. Enough said.
2) against Aberdeen in the Scottish Cup Final (also 1978). Although Rangers 'only' won 2-1, the teams were actually worlds apart, with the Ibrox club in almost complete control. 'Man of the Match' Russell was a joy to watch, his vision and class in midfield illuminating the game.

Strangely enough, the player never featured for Scotland. On the occasions when he was chosen, injury always prevented an actual appearance. In 1987, after some ten years in Govan, he joined Motherwell, where success also greeted him.

To this day, he is still held in great affection in both those areas of the country and maybe, even, in a particular corner of Holland known as Eindhoven.

Rangers Career Statistics
Games: 370 Goals: 46 League Championship Medals: 1
Scottish Cup Medals: 3 League Cup Medals: 4

DEREK PARLANE

Some families are born to football. Three of the Parlane brothers from Rhu all played for Dumbarton, whilst another, inside-forward Jimmy, wore the blue of Rangers for a couple of seasons after the Second World War. Some twenty-five years later, wearing the same colours, his own son would be idolised down Govan way.

Derek Parlane was signed as a midfield player from Queen's park in 1970 and made his debut, away to Falkirk, on 1 January 1971, when Rangers lost 3-1. In only his fifth start for the club, deputising for injured skipper John Greig, he faced the might of Bayern Munich in the semi-final, second leg of the European Cup Winners' Cup at Ibrox in front of an 80,000 crowd. Parlane not only played a 'stormer' but also claimed his side's second goal in the 2-0 victory, volleying home from the edge of the box midway through the first-half. Such an important strike and this his first goal for Rangers.

Early on in Season 1972/73, manager Jock Wallace 'converted' him to a striker (he was good in the air and on the ground) and that was that. Parlane netted nineteen times in twenty-nine games to become top scorer in the league campaign and then, on Scottish Cup Final day, struck Rangers' first in the famous 3-2 victory over Celtic. Although there was no silverware for the 'Light Blues' the following year, the new-born 'hit-man' entered the record books when he scored the Ibrox club's 6000th league goal, 'away' to Hearts in mid-January. Incidentally, Parlane claimed all four for Rangers that day in the 4-2 result and indeed, would prove to be his side's top scorer in four out of five seasons during that period.

When nine years of Celtic supremacy was finally over and the Championship regained at Easter Road in March 1975, the striker's contribution of sixteen league goals had included five in the 6-1 demolition of Dunfermline the previous October. As well as playing for his country twelve times, Derek won another two Championships (1975/76 and 1977/78), one Scottish Cup (1978/79) and three League Cups (1975/76, 1977/78 and 1978/79) with Rangers, before joining Leeds United in March 1980 for £160,000. His travels would take him on to both Hong Kong and Belgium in due course, as well as appearing for Manchester City when Billy McNeill was in charge.

It is pleasing for a family to watch a son follow in his father's footsteps to Ibrox. It is even more satisfying to see that son achieve greatness in the blue. Derek Parlane did that.

Rangers Career Statistics
Games: 300 Goals: 111 League Championship Medals: 3
Scottish Cup Medals: 2 League Cup Medals: 3

Mitre

RALPH BRAND

anager, Bill Struth, obviously saw a great deal to appreciate whilst watching the schoolboy international between England and Scotland on television in 1952, as one speedy youngster was immediately signed on provisional forms. This naturally suited the Edinburgh boy, because all he ever wanted to be in life was a footballer. Some two-and-a-half years later, in November 1954, Ralph Brand, not quite eighteen, scored twice on his Rangers debut in the 6-0 league demolition of Kilmarnock. A goal-scorer supreme in the making.

Following two years' National Service, he netted eleven times in twenty-two league games during Season 1957/58. Twelve months on, the statistics were only three more games played but an additional ten goals. By Season 1960/61, the famous Millar/Brand scoring partnership was in full flow, with the duo claiming thirty-three league strikes between them as Rangers lifted a Scottish League and League Cup 'double'. Indeed, the players had struck a chord together back in the first official outing of Season 1959/60, when, in a League Cup section match, they netted five between them as Hibernian were routed 6-1.

A deadly penalty-box player, Ralph Brand's record is really quite staggering - 206 goals in 317 games. When Rangers beat Dundee 3-1 on 25 April,1964, he became the first footballer to score in three successive Scottish Cup Finals, following his goals against St.Mirren (2-0, 21.4.62) and Celtic (3-0, 15.5.63). He actually hit a 'double' in the 'Old Firm' Final of 1963. Additionally, Brand netted six times in seven Cup Finals with the 'Light Blues' and was never on the losing side. Some record for some player!

In May 1961, he was part of that team from Govan which, entering the history books to become the first British club to reach the final of a European competition, came so close to glory. Along the way, the scalps of Ferencvaros, Borussia Möenchengladbach and Wolves were collected. The striker not only scored against all of them but claimed a 'hat-trick' against the Germans in the quarter-finals.

During those halcyon days of the early sixties, the player was unfairly dismissed in some quarters as just a poacher. A much more accurate and realistic appraisal of his career would simply be : Ralph Brand, a goalscoring Rangers legend.

Rangers Career Statistics

Games: 317 Goals: 206 League Championship Medals: 4
Scottish Cup Medals: 3 League Cup Medals: 4

JOHN BROWN

Sometimes it is an unlikely hero who emerges from the sidelines to take centre stage at a crucial period of any Championship. Take the case of John Brown. The player with a Rangers heart started Season 1995/96 in his capacity as reserve coach, with the possibility of regular first-team action seemingly rather remote. Although he had taken his place in the starting line-up on one occasion prior to the turn of the year (against Juventus at Ibrox in the November 'Champions League' clash), this was only due to Alan McLaren's suspension for that game.

The New Year, however, toasted a new set of circumstances. The 'Light Blues' faced the intimidating prospect of two extremely tough away games in succession - Aberdeen (February 25) and then Hibernian (March 3), with skipper, Richard Gough, missing through injury for at least the trip north. Enter 'Bomber'. John played superbly that day at the heart of the defence. His contribution to the 1-0 victory was quite significant, even managing a goal-line clearance to deny the Dons an equaliser. The following week saw the return of Gough but he had to be substituted at half-time, injured in an extremely physical and bruising encounter. Enter 'Bomber'. Once again, a solid performance beside McLaren and Petric at the back.

The defender arrived at Ibrox from Dundee in January 1988 for a fee of £350,000. By the following season, he was a regular in Graeme Souness' team. Brown had actually made his mark some years earlier, when he struck the only goal of the game at Ibrox, ensuring a Dundee cup triumph in February 1985. This was followed by a hat-trick at Dens Park, when Rangers were beaten 3-2 in November 1985. At least that couldn't happen again!

When the team came so close to European glory in Season 1992/93, 'Bomber' was there. It will be a long time before the emotional aftermath of Rangers' final 'Champions League' game at Ibrox against CSKA Moscow is forgotten. Few who were present that night, will ever forget the sight of John Brown throwing his jersey to fans in the enclosure.

A first domestic 'treble' since 1978 was also achieved that year. Our hero pulled on the blue 39 times that term, a total only matched by David Robertson. Sadly, as with several other players from the first-team squad, injury played a major role in the early part of 1993/94. All the same, 'Bomber' did provide one awesome moment of genuine satisfaction - his only goal of the season, certainly, but surely one of the year's most memorable. In the second half of what was proving to be a most difficult quarter-final Scottish Cup tie, John unleashed a devastatingly ferocious left-foot strike, from some thirty yards, to open the scoring and send Rangers and not opponents, Hearts, on their way to Hampden.

The player never gave less than 100%, even on those occasions when taking the field carrying a strain or injury. In fact, prior to the title decider against Aberdeen at Ibrox (11.5.91), he needed injections before kick-off just to start the match. With twenty minutes of the game remaining, a ruptured achilles tendon ended his involvement. It must be said, however, that John returned for the party with the aid of crutches.

Footballers who genuinely play for the jersey are now a rare breed, a dying breed. Maybe another John Brown will emerge from the shadows but that, in truth, is highly unlikely.

Rangers Career Statistics
Games: 278 Goals: 18 League Championship Medals: 6
Scottish Cup Medals: 3 League Cup Medals: 3

ALEX SCOTT

angers and Everton have forged something of a relationship over the last few years. Gary Stevens, Trevor Steven and Stuart McCall all headed north to play supporting roles on the stage that was to become 'Nine-in-a Row', whilst later, Maurice Johnston, Duncan Ferguson and Alex Cleland took the road south, swapping the blue of Glasgow for the blue of Liverpool. Before all this, however, another talented Ranger had arrived on Merseyside at a time when four young men with decidedly strange haircuts were about to conquer the world.......back in 1963.

As a winger, Alex Scott had it all - he was powerful, very fast, an excellent crosser and a quite superb finisher. In March 1955, he scored a hat-trick at Ibrox when Falkirk were beaten 4-1. Still only a teenager, it was his first game for Rangers. The following week, in a friendly match with the mighty Arsenal at Highbury, Scott netted twice in the 3-3 draw. The nation took note.

By 28 April 1956, and season's end, the 'Light Blues' were Champions again. Scott had made the No.7 jersey his own and the fans accepted him as a natural successor to the legendary Willie Waddell, who wore the same number with so much distinction in Rangers' first great post-war team.

Another three Championships (1957, 1959 and 1961) were supplemented by a Scottish Cup (1960) and two League Cups (1960 and1961). The league title race of Season 1960/61 brought about another milestone in Rangers' proud and distinguished history - the club's 5000th league goal. The scorer? Alex Scott - and on the last day of the campaign, when a 7-3 win over Ayr United guaranteed the flag by a narrow-one-point margin from second-placed Kilmarnock. That year, the Light Blues' became the first British team to reach a European final. Although Fiorentina proved too strong over two legs (aggregate 4-1), Scott not only scored in the Italian 2nd leg but also against Borussia Moenchengladbach and Wolves, in the quarter-finals and semi-finals of the tournament respectively.

Capped sixteen times for Scotland (eleven when with Rangers), he was certainly one of the dark blue heroes when the national side recorded that famous 2-0 triumph at Hampden in 1962, the first win in official internationals against England for 25 years. Interestingly, the winger's younger brother James (of Hibernian) also played for his country.

Following the emergence of Willie Henderson, Rangers' other famous outside-right of the period, Alex Scott joined Everton in February,1963. He would go on to win both Championship and Cup honours with the English giants, endlessly entertaining and enthralling another passionate support in blue.

Rangers Career Statistics
Games: 331 Goals: 108 League Championship Medals: 4
Scottish Cup Medals: 1 League Cup Medals: 2

JIM BAXTER

The orchestra had found its conductor in Jim Baxter. Touched by genius, surely and (maybe just) the most naturally gifted Ranger of them all. The signing of this immense talent was, in many ways, the completion of a jigsaw and a good team would become great.

When manager Scot Symon brought the player to Ibrox in the summer of 1960, a Scottish record fee of £17,500 was paid to Raith Rovers. Almost immediately, 'Slim Jim' became an integral part of the Rangers squad that would dominate Scottish football for some four to five years. Even today, that side of the early sixties is still considered to be one of the greatest in the club's long and illustrious history.

Celtic were waiting at Parkhead in only the second league game of Season 1960/61. By crushing them 5-1, Rangers recorded one of their most impressive victories at that venue and set off confidently on the road to the Championship. Although there was no league title the following year, the Scottish and League Cups were both on show in the Trophy Room. Season 1962/63 saw a League and Scottish Cup 'double' with a glorious 'triple crown' in place by the following year, when Celtic were beaten no less than five times in five meetings. During the period 1960-65, Jim Baxter faced up to Celtic on no less than eighteen occasions, tasting the bitterness of defeat only twice.

Worshipped both for his supreme left-foot skills and 'Mickey-taking' abilities, midfielder Baxter truly excelled in the heat of 'Old Firm' infernos - this was his stage. The Scottish Cup Final of 1963 (the first involving the old rivals for thirty-five years) was a case in point.

After a 1-1 draw in the first game, a crowd of 120,000 gathered for the replay. Still recalled as one of the most one-sided finals ever, Rangers turned on the style with tormentor-in-chief, 'Slim Jim', orchestrating from midfield. The 3-0 scoreline hardly conveyed blue superiority on the day and with some twenty minutes still remaining, the green and white fans deserted the Hampden slopes en masse having seen and suffered enough. Celtic had merely been the audience to a Baxter performance, although no applause was forthcoming.

In the dark blue of Scotland, he was just as much a revelation, with two shows in particular standing out - both against England. At Wembley in 1963, he not only tormented the life out of those conceited white shirts but also netted both his country's goals in a 2-1 win. Four years later, it was even more satisfying, when the recently crowned World Champions were beaten 3-2, with Baxter again reigning supreme at the carnival and scoring twice into the bargain. The player earned 34 Scotland 'Caps' in total.

After early success in Season 1964/65 (Jim captained Rangers to a 2-1 League Cup Final victory over Celtic), tragedy struck further afield in Europe when, late on in the game with Rapid of Vienna, he suffered a leg break. In May 1965, the player joined Sunderland. Two and a half years later, it was a move to Nottingham Forest for £100,000. Jim Baxter returned to Rangers in May of 1969 (on a free transfer) but was released by manager, Willie Waddell, at the end of that season after just one year.

His days with Rangers were finally over but the legend that is Jim Baxter lives on. Of one thing there is no doubt, we will never see his like again.

Rangers Career Statistics
Games: 254 Goals: 24 League Championship Medals: 3
Scottish Cup Medals: 3 League Cup Medals: 4

BOBBY SHEARER

As John Brown is to the eighties and nineties, so was Bobby Shearer to the fifties and sixties. In other words, a player so committed to the cause that the Rangers jersey is everything and playing for the club is the ultimate.

Arriving in Govan from Hamilton in 1955, Shearer would soon form a famous full-back partnership with Eric Caldow, who had joined Rangers some two years earlier. The fiery redhead made his debut, 'away' to Airdrie (28 January 1956), in a 4-0 'Light Blue' victory on the road to that year's Championship. The No.2 shirt would be worn with distinction for almost a decade, in which time another five league titles (1956/57, 1958/59, 1960/61, 1962/63 and 1963/64) plus three Scottish Cups (1961/62, 1962/63 and 1963/64) and four League Cups (1960/61, 1961/62, 1963/64 and 1964/65) took their place in the Ibrox Trophy Room.

In due course, the player became club captain and earned the nickname 'Captain Cutlass', such was the ferocity of his tackling. Few wingers relished Shearer as an opponent, for obvious reasons! During his Rangers career, Shearer, at one point, played an amazing 165 games in succession and became only the second man (after George Young) to captain his side to a glorious 'treble' of the Championship and both domestic Cups.

In 1965, after ten years and 407 games (and let's not forget the four goals!), Bobby Shearer's time in the blue came to an end but not his love affair with the club. To this day, he remains as much a Rangers man as he ever was. True and Blue.

Rangers Career Statistics
Games : 407 Goals : 4 League Championship Medals : 5
Scottish Cup Medals : 3 League Cup Medals : 4

BILLY SIMPSON

With hindsight, there is always a turning point in any League Championship race, when the wind changes. One particular game, following which, supporters just knew that all was either won or lost. A prime example, in modern Rangers history, would be the Ne'erday encounter with Celtic at Ibrox on 1 January 1987, when Souness and his team played with such swaggering belief and conviction that their visitors were delivered a crushing psychological blow. Despite a healthy lead in the title race at that time, the tide had turned for the Parkhead club and Rangers would be crowned Champions in due course. An even earlier example had happened back in April 1957, when a certain Belfast lad and his team-mates were on a day trip to Edinburgh.

Billy Simpson always wanted to play for Rangers and his wish came true in October 1950, when the Ibrox club paid a record £11,500 fee to Linfield for the striker's services. In only his third game (against East Fife in the 5-0 league victory), he scored a 'hat-trick' and by Season 1952/53, Simpson had netted twenty-one Championship goals in the same number of games. Rangers won the 'double' of League and Scottish Cup that year and, indeed, it was the Irishman's solitary strike in the Cup Final replay (against Aberdeen) that ensured the trophy was Govan bound. Amazingly, a crowd of over 129,000 watched the first Hampden match (a 1-1 draw) with the team from the north but 'only' 113,700 turned out for the second meeting four days later!

Just like Willie Thornton immediately before him, Simpson was absolutely deadly in the air, with bravery enough to spare. Even in those areas where the boots were flying, he never held back and pursued scoring chances with the head regardless of thought for his own well-being. The courageous player was top-scorer with twenty-eight domestic goals in Season 1954/55, although only the Glasgow Charity Cup was welcomed to the Trophy Room. Despite claiming ten league strikes the following year, when the Championship was regained, it was late on in the next again season (1956/57) that a Simpson goal turned the race decisively in Rangers' favour as highlighted above.

Hearts had led the title race for most of the campaign, playing with confidence and assurance. By mid April, with only five games remaining, Rangers were due at Tynecastle, still chasing the Edinburgh side. Obviously, something had to give. Billy Simpson's goal that day (in the 1-0 victory) not only won the game but also seemed to crush Hearts' spirit and self-belief by much more than just the loss of two points. By season's end, the 'Light Blues' were celebrating another League Championship.

Later that year (in October 1957), the Tynecastle club featured once again in Simpson's career, when he scored his 100th Rangers goal against them. Earning twelve 'Caps' for Northern Ireland, the player netted the winner in the 1957 Wembley clash with England, as his country secured a famous 3-2 triumph. He left Rangers in the spring of 1959 (having scored 163 goals) to join Stirling Albion for a reported fee of £6000.

Rangers Career Statistics
Games: 239 Goals: 163 League Championship Medals: 3
Scottish Cup Medals: 1

JERRY DAWSON

Long before a certain 'Prince of Denmark' achieved heroic status wearing the blue, there was another 'Prince' down Ibrox way. He was a goalkeeper one of the finest ever to come out of Scotland and his name was Jerry Dawson.

Manager Bill Struth saw genuine potential at an early age and signed the Falkirk youngster from Camelon Juniors in 1929. By the latter part of Season 1932/33, he was established as first choice in the Rangers side. Not particularly tall for a 'keeper (but then again, neither was Andy Goram),his greatest strengths were lightning reflexes and the ability totally to dominate his penalty area. Dawson was also very brave and had the uncanny knack of being able to psyche out opposition forwards.

The player's honours with Rangers were many. In a career spanning some sixteen years, he won five League Championships, two Scottish Cups, two Scottish War Cups, two Summer War Cups and one Southern League Cup. The 'keeper also appeared for his country on fourteen separate occasions.

At the beginning and end of his Ibrox career, two very different games conveyed the extremes that football can offer. In his very first 'Old Firm' encounter of September 1931, the Celtic goalkeeper, John Thomson, was injured in an accidental clash with Rangers forward, Sam English and later died. Some fourteen years on, as the world celebrated the defeat of Nazism, the Russians of Moscow Dynamo enthralled a crowd of 90,000 at Ibrox in one of the most famous games ever played in Scotland. Jerry Dawson kept goal that day for Rangers, in what was to be his last ever appearance for the club.

After playing for Falkirk and managing East Fife, he then worked as a journalist. Jerry Dawson died on 19 January 1977.

No doubt, most of the current crop of fans would be surprised to know that there was, indeed, 'Prince' before Brian Laudrup. Thankfully the Dane didn't play between the posts otherwise another adopted name would have been called for. The title, 'Prince of Goalkeepers', was already taken.

Rangers Career Statistics
Games : 271 Goals : Nil League Championship Medals : 5
Scottish Cup Medals : 2

IAN McCOLL

Ian McColl was one of football's great achievers, not only winning numerous trophies with Rangers (thirteen in all) but also successfully managing Scotland to great effect in the 1960s, when his playing days were over.

The seventeen-year-old arrived at the club in June 1945, from Queen's Park and made his first-team debut against Partick Thistle in the 4-2, August league victory. A 'part-timer' throughout his Ibrox career, the hard-tackling wing-half would soon go on to fill the position vacated by Scot Symon (another uncompromising player) in what was to become that famous post-war 'Iron Curtain' defence. With so many legends in the Rangers team back then (Young, Woodburn, Waddell and Thornton, to name but four), it must have seemed like a football academy made in heaven for the young man.

The honours came fast and furious - a League and League Cup 'double' in 1946/47, a Scottish Cup in 1947/48 and then, Scotland's first ever domestic 'treble' of the Championship and both Cups in 1948/49. McColl would go on to win another four titles and three Scottish Cups with Rangers, serving the club for fifteen years in 526 games. There was also the small matter of fourteen Scotland 'Caps' and remember, all this whilst still a civil engineer during the day!

Near the end of his Ibrox days, one particular game stands out. Due to an injury to Harold Davis, the player was recalled for the Scottish Cup Final of 1960, when Kilmarnock awaited at Hampden. Despite having appeared in only five games that season (all in the League), McColl was immense, winning ball after ball in midfield, as Rangers lifted the trophy on a 2-0 scoreline. After leaving Ibrox, he managed Scotland for some four and a half years, winning sixteen games out of twenty-seven fixtures for the national side. Then it was the North-East of England and Sunderland for three years, before finally walking away from football.

The Rangers career of Ian McColl proudly stands comparison with that of John Greig. Nothing else really needs to be said.

Rangers Career Statistics
Games: 526 Goals: 14 League Championship Medals: 6
Scottish Cup Medals: 5 League Cup Medals: 2

SANDY JARDINE

angers' disastrous Scottish Cup exit at the hands of lowly Berwick happened on 27 January 1967. One week later, an eighteen-year-old Edinburgh lad made his debut at Ibrox in the 5-1 mauling of Hearts. Both these events are significant episodes in the history of Glasgow Rangers Football Club; the first for more obvious reasons and the second because that youngster would, in time, develop into one of the country's finest, most cultured full-backs.

Initially, Sandy Jardine (actually, William but the colour of his hair decided the name) was utilised in various defensive positions but by the end of Season 1970/71, the No. 2 jersey and right-back position was his. Fast and strong, Jardine played the game with a cool elegance and fairness. His first Scottish honour, the League Cup of October 1970, was followed by glory on the European front when the 'Light Blues' lifted the 1972 Cup Winners' Cup in Spain. Indeed, it was the player's first-minute goal at Ibrox, in the semi-final against the mighty Bayern Munich, that set Rangers on the path to victory and the road to Barcelona. Sweet retribution for Jardine, as he had suffered at the hands of the German giants back in 1967, when the teutonic side lifted the silverware following the Nuremberg final of the same competition.

Back on home soil, the Championship was won in 1974/75 (with Sandy netting nine times) and then the Trophy Room welcomed all three domestic prizes in both 1976 and 1978. By this time, the player had formed an impressive full-back partnership with Danny McGrain (of Celtic) in the dark blue of his country. Winning 38 Scotland 'Caps', Jardine appeared at both the 1974 and 1978 World Cup Finals in Germany and Argentina respectively. Along with Brian Laudrup, he is one of a very select band to have been named 'Player of the Year' twice by the Scottish Football Writers' Association'. On the second occasion, he had reached the ripe old age of thirty-eight.

After the Scottish Cup Final of 1982, Jardine joined Hearts and as sweeper, was part of the Gorgie team that very nearly achieved a famous League and Scottish Cup 'double'. His 1,000th senior game (a first in Scotland) was with the Edinburgh side when they met Rangers on league duty in November 1985 . . . and duly won 3-0! In time, the player would return to Ibrox working on the commercial side of the operation.

Back in 1967, when Rangers lost the European Cup Winners' Cup to Bayern Munich, a certain Franz Beckenbauer praised Jardine's overall performance that night. Maybe small consolation at the time but it should have come as no suprise, therefore, that such a glittering and illustrious career lay ahead for one William 'Sandy' Jardine.

Rangers Career Statistics
Games: 674 Goals: 77 League Championship Medals: 3
Scottish Cup Medals: 5 League Cup Medals: 5
European Medals: 1

TORRY GILLICK

Few players are given the opportunity of returning to Rangers after seeking pastures new. Fewer still were allowed to wear the blue for a second time when Bill Struth was manager of the club. A notable exception was Torry Gillick.

The inside-forward arrived at Ibrox in 1933 from Petershill Juniors, prior to his eighteenth birthday. By April 1935, he had won his first senior honour, when Rangers lifted the Scottish Cup after beating Hamilton 2-1 at Hampden. Torry had played in every round of the competition, netting four times on the road to the final.

By December of that same year, he was on his way to Everton, who paid £8000 (a club record transfer fee) for his services. Certainly this was a 'king's ransom' in those days but, in time, it proved to be an astute buy for the Liverpool club. Indeed, the player was a huge success in England and Everton were crowned Champions in 1939. During the Second World War, Gillick 'guested' for both Rangers and Airdrie. The legendary Stanley Matthews also wore the colours (twice) in this period and won a Glasgow Charity Cup medal in the process!

Mr. Struth brought his man back to Rangers in 1945, as the world tried to return to some sort of normality. When Rangers played the touring Moscow Dynamo in November that year, it was Torry who pointed out that, at one point during this famous 'friendly' game, the Russians actually had a team of twelve on the park.

His right-wing partnership with Willie Waddell was a lethal cocktail and the combination of Gillick's through passes and Waddell's subsequent crosses proved quite irresistable. A domestic 'double' of the Championship and League Cup was secured in Season 1946/47. As well as netting twelve goals in that league campaign, he also scored in the final of the League Cup when Aberdeen were soundly beaten, 4-0.

The Scottish Cup of 1947/48 and the League Cup of 1948/49 were his last honours with Rangers and the player ended his football career at Firhill with Partick Thistle.

Torry Gillick was only 56 when he died in the December of 1971. 'The Wee Blue Devil', Alan Morton, passed away the very same day. Legends both.

Rangers Career Statistics
Games: 140 Goals: 62 League Championship Medals: 2
Scottish Cup Medals: 2 League Cup Medals: 2

JOHNNY HUBBARD

Whenever Rangers were awarded a penalty-kick in the 1950s, the fans immediately celebrated an actual goal. The reason? A diminutive South African, only 5 foot 4 inches in height and less than 9 stones in weight, named Johnny Hubbard. The Jorg Albertz of his day........except for the small matter of body size!

Hubbard arrived at Ibrox from Pretoria in July 1949, for a trial with the club, on the recommendation of ex-Hibernian player Alex Prior, who was then a photographer in the country. Manager Bill Struth's initial doubts about the little winger were soon overcome and he signed for Rangers. It didn't take long for him to become a firm favourite with the fans.

Though the 'wee man' scored over 100 times for his team during a 238 game career, it is as the undisputed penalty-king of Scottish Foootball that he is most fondly remembered. Johnny netted 65 times from 68 spot-kicks during that period including a quite staggering 23 consecutive strikes from 1949 to the end of January 1956. It was 'keeper Dave Walker of Airdrie who ended that amazing sequence although our friend did indeed score in Rangers 4-0 victory. Incidentally, only two other goalkeepers in Scotland were successful in stopping one of those penalty specials - Jimmy Brown of Kilmarnock and Bert Slater of Falkirk.

The history books record that Johnny Hubbard also has another two unique claims to fame :
1) In Rangers 1955 'Ne'erday' tussle with Celtic, the winger not only scored a 'hat-trick' in the 4-1 triumph but netted all three goals in the final fifteen minutes of play. Yes, one was a penalty.
2) He scored for South Africa against Scotland at Ibrox.

Johnny Hubbard left Rangers and joined Bury in April 1959 for £6,000. Goalkeepers throughout Scotland breathed a collective sigh of relief.

Rangers Career Statistics
Games : 238 Goals : 106 League Championship Medals : 3
Scottish Cup Medals : 1

JIM FORREST

Inconceivable as it may seem, there was a time back in the swinging sixties when a certain centre-forward was dismissed in many quarters as a player who 'could only score goals!'

In case this brings to mind someone like Marco Negri from Rangers' most recent past, it should be stressed that the striker in question from that era was much more accomplished. Fast, brave, good in the air, superbly balanced and a deadly finisher with either foot, Jim Forrest scored 145 goals in 163 games for the club and was one of only a select band of players to claim 100 in the league. Additionally, Season 1964/65 saw the player net 57 goals in all competitions - a record that still stands to this day.

Forrest joined Rangers as a schoolboy, before being 'farmed out' to Drumchapel Amateurs in Glasgow. Back at Ibrox with his 'old' club, the player was soon amongst the goals and the honours. A glorious 'treble' was secured in 1963/64, with Jim striking no fewer than 39 times. The League Cup Final of October 1963, when Morton were overwhelmed 5-0, proved to be a rather unique and historical event, with the Forrest family well to the fore. Not only had our hero struck a record four times but his cousin, Alec Willoughby, claimed the fifth! The following year, when Rangers retained the League Cup, Jim not only scored twice in the 2-1 semi-final win over Dundee United but he also netted both goals in the final itself, when Celtic surrendered by the same scoreline.

However, in the aftermath of the 'Light Blues' humiliating exit at the hands of Berwick in the Scottish Cup (January 1967), scapegoats were required. The blame, unfairly, landed at the feet of both Jim and inside-forward, George McLean. Neither kicked a ball in earnest for the club again, with the gentlemanly Forrest joining Preston North End in March for £38,000.

It seemed obvious, even at the time, that Rangers had made a major error in transferring the player in such haste. This rush to judgement may just have cost them the European Cup Winners' Cup two months later in Nuremberg, when any natural striker in blue seemed conspicuous by his absence.

Postscript: A rather tenuous link with their 'old' club did re-emerge some years later, when, in the twiiight of their careers, cousins Jim and Alec played for Hong Kong . . . Rangers

Rangers Career Statistics
Games : 163 Goals : 145 League Championship Medals : 1
League Cup Medals : 2

TOM FORSYTH

ost Rangers players tend to remember their first goal for the club, even though it may have come during an end-of-season encounter when little of importance was at stake. Consider the case of Tom Forsyth. Certainly, his first strike was registered at that time of the year but maybe because it happened to be the winning goal in an 'Old Firm' Cup Final, more than just minor interest value was attached to it. Especially by a crowd of nearly 123,000.

Initially signed as a midfielder from Motherwell in October 1972, manager Jock Wallace saw him as more of a defender (he was a quite superb tackler) and before too long, Forsyth and Colin Jackson were the beating heart of that very successful Rangers team of the seventies. So successful, in fact, that domestic 'trebles' were celebrated down Ibrox way in two out of three seasons between 1975 and 1978. For Forsyth, these glories were still some way off but at the end of his first season, there was the Centenary Scottish Cup Final. Quite soon, his name would be on everyone's lips.

Rangers had beaten Dundee United, Hibernian, Airdrie and Ayr United on the road to Hampden although it took two games to dispose of Hibs, with nearly 64,000 at Ibrox to witness the initial 1-1 draw and just over 49,000 at Easter Road to see Rangers win the replay 2-1. Celtic were the final hurdle, in what was to be a hugely entertaining game on May 5 at Hampden. Kenny Dalglish drew first blood before Derek Parlane headed the equaliser ten minutes before the break, and then Alfie Conn's early second-half goal was cancelled out by a Connelly penalty. With the score level at 2-2, Tom Forsyth's time had come. Derek Johnstone's header, from an inch-perfect Tommy McLean free-kick, seemed net-bound before striking a post and rolling along the goal-line. After hitting the other post, the ball appeared to stop. Forsyth was the first to react and, from all of six inches, scored for Rangers, securing victory by the odd goal in five.

'Big Tam' played for his country twenty-two times and was a member of Scotland's World Cup Finals squad in 1978. After retiring in March 1982, due to injury, he entered football management and with Tommy McLean, led Motherwell to the Scottish Cup in 1991.

Tom Forsyth actually netted six times during his Rangers career. No prizes for guessing which goal is recalled the most. By him or the 'Bears' of Ibrox.

Rangers Career Statistics
Games: 326 Goals: 6 League Championship Medals: 3
Scottish Cup Medals: 4 League Cup Medals: 2

ERIC CALDOW

t is rare for a Rangers footballer to play alongside giants from two different eras during his time at the club. When a certain youthful Ayrshire full-back made his debut in 1953, legends such as Woodburn, Waddell and Young wore the blue and then, in the early sixties, Baxter, McMillan and Wilson were his contemporaries. Exalted company indeed but, right from the start, Eric Caldow never looked out of place.

Within one year of arriving at the club from Muirkirk Juniors, he was a team member and an exceptional Ibrox career had begun. Wingers would rarely pass him, such was his speed of thought and action. He was very fast, in both senses. Following his first Championship at the end of Season 1955/56, Caldow was part of the 'Light Blue' line-up that faced Nice in Rangers first ever European Cup game. As captain, he was also there, in May 1961, when his team became the first British club to reach the final of any European competition. Opponents, Fiorentina of Italy, however, proved just too strong on that occasion.

On the domestic front, further Championships followed in 1957, 1959, 1961 and 1963, with two Scottish Cups (1960 and 1962) and three League Cups (Seasons 1960/61, 1961/62 and 1964/65). Ten major honours in total.

His career in the dark blue was just as impressive. As well as captaining his country, he only missed two Scotland internationals in the period April 1957 to April 1963. Indeed, the defender was the first Rangers player to appear in the World Cup Finals. Tragically, after only some few minutes play at Wembley in 1963, his leg was broken in three places after a tackle from England's Bobby Smith. Caldow had played forty times for Scotland, twenty-nine at right-back, with the other eleven on the left side of the field.

His Ibrox career ended in April 1966 after 407 games for Rangers. In all that time, Eric Caldow was never once booked.

Rangers Career Statistics
Games : 407 Goals : 25 League Championship Medals : 5
Scottish Cup Medals : 2 League Cup Medals : 3

IAN McMILLAN

angers were struggling at the start of Season 1958/59, with only one win (and two defeats) in their first five games. The Ibrox club had won nothing the previous year and another barren period seemed in prospect. At the time, few imagined that the arrival of a twenty-seven-year-old part-timer would halt the decline, let alone transform the team into Champions. But Ian McMillan a very special seven-year-old part-timer.

The inside-forward had already played for Scotland five times (during his ten years with Airdrie) before signing for Rangers on 2 October 1958 and in his very first game, scored in the 4-4 'home' draw with Raith Rovers. The Govan team then embarked on a title-winning run, losing only once in twenty-three matches, before lifting the trophy (by two points from Hearts) the following April. Ian McMillan had played in twenty-six games, netting eight times and was the true creative force behind that Championship success, even though he remained a part-time player, returning to his 'other job' as a chartered surveyor during the week. His nickname of the 'Wee Prime Minister' (after Conservative Prime Minister, Harold MacMillan) was most appropriate; after all, he did control affairs......on the park.

With the arrival of Jim Baxter in the summer of 1960, the most gifted and visionary duo in Scotland were now wearing the blue and one of the truly great Rangers teams was complete. It was on the European stage, the season immediately following that MacMillan truly excelled, as Rangers became the first British team to reach the final of the Cup Winners' Cup although Fiorentina proved too strong at the last hurdle.

A 'double' of League and League Cup was, however, celebrated in 1960/61, with both Cups heading for the Trophy Room one year on. Then it was the Championship and Scottish Cup (in 1962/63) before the ultimate glory of a domestic 'treble' in 1964. Ian McMillan played his last game for Rangers on 29 April 1964, against St. Johnstone, at the end of that wonderful season, before returning to his first love, Airdrie, in the December.

Even after all these years, the 'Wee Prime Minister' still holds a special place in the hearts and minds of those down Ibrox way.

Rangers Career Statistics
Games: 194 Goals: 55 League Championship Medals: 2
Scottish Cup Medals: 3 League Cup Medals: 2

BOB MacPHAIL

ne of the most impressive exhibits in the Ibrox Trophy Room is a small cabinet, some 18 inches wide, which contains the finest collection of medals to be found in Scotland. Thirty-six in all, including seven for the Scottish Cup, they were all won by the great inside-left, Bob McPhail, the last of manager Bill Struth's Ibrox legends from the days when Rangers players, to a man, arrived at 'away' grounds wearing blue suit, white shirt, blue overcoat (with velvet collar), black shoes and socks, all set of with the compulsory bowler hat!

Bob joined Rangers from Airdrie in 1927 for the princely sum of £4,500 after having struck 74 goals for the Lanarkshire club. Two weeks earlier, he had worn the dark blue for the very first time, when Scotland played England at the National Stadium. It was with Airdrie, in fact, that he won the first of his Scottish Cup winners' medals, when they defeated Hibernian 2-0, lifting the trophy for the only time in their history. Indeed, this was the last Scottish Cup Final to be held at Ibrox until Kilmarnock and Falkirk headed there in the early summer of 1997, due to the unavailability of Hampden.

Almost immediately, at his new club, McPhail established a daunting left-wing partnership with the original 'Wee Blue Devil', Alan Morton. At the end of that first full season (1927/28), a League and Cup 'double' was being hailed in Govan for the very first time. In April, the 'Light Blues' had smashed their Scottish Cup hoodoo by lifting the trophy for the first time in twenty-five years, following the acclaimed 4-0 rout of Celtic.

Bob scored Rangers' second that day and went on to strike an amazing purple patch at this last stage of the tournament by netting in the finals of 1932 (3-0 v. Kilmarnock.), 1934 (5-0 v. St. Mirren) and 1936 (1-0 v. Third Lanark). It should be noted that the club also claimed the trophy in 1930 and 1935 but McPhail was not on the scoresheet! His number of Scottish Cup medals is shared by the Celtic duo, Billy McNeill and Jimmy McMenemy but it is Charles Campbell of Queen's Park who holds the record, with eight.

'Greetin' Boab', as he was called, also won nine League Championship, six Charity Cup and five Glasgow Cup awards in his time at Ibrox. His record also shows a tally of 230 league goals whilst wearing the royal blue and 70 in a previous life with Airdrie. And the story behind the nickname? Seemingly, he barracked Torry Gillick during a game, suggesting that the player may just want to get on with the match instead of being too concerned about an injury. The name stuck.

Although winning 17 Scotland 'Caps', the player's collection could actually have been increased to 20 but for the timely intervention of Mr. Struth. Having been chosen by his country on three separate occasions to face England at Wembley, the player withdrew prior to each game. Rangers were in the Scottish Cup Final for each of those years and as the Hampden match was scheduled for the week after the International, advice that club should always come first was accepted without question.

Bob McPhail retired in 1941 but to this day, can still be seen on match days, sitting in the Directors' Box at Ibrox. A true 'Living Legend'.

Rangers Career Statistics
Games: 408 Goals: 261 League Championship Medals: 9
Scottish Cup Medals: 6

KAI JOHANSEN

Some memories never fade, let alone die and the vision remains like a newly developed photograph. One such recollection, for those who follow, is of a Dane in blue leaving a twenty-five yard track of scorched earth on the Hampden turf and becoming the first foreign player to score the winning goal in a Scottish Cup Final.

In many ways, Kai Johansen was a full-back ahead of his time at Ibrox. Manager Scot Symon's policy of defenders not crossing the halfway line certainly did not suit the Dane's European style of attacking play and it, therefore, took time to adapt to these restrictions following his transfer from Morton prior to Season 1965/66.

Rangers and Celtic met in the League Cup Final of October 1965. Celtic won 2-1, with their star left-winger, John Hughes, coming out top in his duel with Johansen. The two faced up to each other again six months later, at the same ground, in another final – but this time the outcome, both individually and collectively, would be so different.

Celtic were firm favourites going into the Scottish Cup Final, having already beaten Rangers 5-1 in their most recent encounter in the league. Following a 0-0 draw at Hampden in the first game, the teams met again four days later for a replay. The stalemate continued until some twenty minutes before the end, when, from the right flank, Kai hit a thunderous twenty-five-yard drive that screamed past Ronnie Simpson, the opposition 'keeper, into the back of the Celtic net. He had capped a marvellous display (Hughes 'hardly kicked a ball' that night) with a goal fit enough to win any major championship.

In five seasons with the club, Johansen played 238 games (scoring 9 goals) but his medal collection remained at one. The full-back was a member of the team that came so close to European glory in 1967, only to lose at the final stage to Bayern Munich. Additionally, he played for Denmark 20 times.

In time, another Dane and fellow Ranger would write his name all over a Scottish Cup Final. Just like his countryman did some thirty years earlier.

Rangers Career Statistics
Games : 238 Goals : 9
Scottish Cup Medals : 1

DAVIE WILSON

Only the foolhardy would ever question the accolades that were showered upon manager Scot Symon's team of the early 1960s. Even now, after all these years, memories of Baxter and McMillan in midfield, Millar and a Brand up front and Scott and Wilson on the wings, never fail to produce a wry smile and knowing nod of the head.

Davie Wilson (all of 5 feet, 6 inches) was probably the finest left-winger to wear the blue since the legendary Alan Morton, back in the 1920s. Like the 'Wee Blue Devil', he also had a sharp eye for goal. Arriving at Ibrox as a teenager via Baillieston Juniors in May 1956, Wilson scored in only his fourth first-team outing, 'away' to Motherwell, the following March. Rangers won 5-2 on their way to retaining the Championship.

When Rangers next claimed the title, in Season 1958/59, Davie appeared fifteen times, netting twice. Two years later and another league flag, the ratio was thirty-four games to nineteen goals, making him second-top scorer behind Ralph Brand, with twenty-four strikes. That May, the men from Govan entered the history books and became the first British club to reach the final of a European competition. Wilson (sometimes called 'The Blond Bombshell') was part of the team that lost 4-1 on aggregate to Fiorentina of Italy.

A place in the record books was waiting for the player, nevertheless, in the unlikeliest of circumstances. Some ten months after that historic final, the 'Light Blues' met Falkirk at Brockville on league duty. The resultant 7-1 thrashing included an amazing six goals credited to Davie Wilson, with the player thus becoming the only post-war Ranger to net so many in a competitive game.

Both Cups, Scottish and League, were won that season, to be followed by a League and Scottish Cup 'double' in 1962/63. The May final saw Rangers defeat old rivals, Celtic, 3-0 after a replay. Wilson was on the scoresheet.

Although he was awarded 22 Scotland Caps overall, most people tend to remember one particular day when Davie wore the dark blue of his country - against England at Wembley in 1963. Following captain Eric Caldow's broken leg after only six minutes, Wilson slotted into the left full-back position as if to the manor born and played, as they say, a 'blinder'. Scotland recorded a famous 2-1 victory, with Jim Baxter scoring both. The previous year, Davie himself had scored Scotland's first against the 'Auld Enemy' at Hampden, as our national side registered the first win in official internationals against England for 25 years.

Somewhat surprisingly, in August 1967, at the age of 28, he joined Dundee United, with Swede, Orjan Persson, moving in the other direction.

Rangers Career Statistics
Games: 373 Goals: 157 League Champioship Medals: 2
Scottish Cup Medals: 5 League Cup Medals: 2

WILLIE WOODBURN

He was at the heart of Rangers' remarkable post-war 'Iron Curtain' defence that included Brown (in goal), Young and Shaw (at full-back) and McColl and Cox (at half-back). He was probably the most talented centre-half ever to wear the blue, yet was suspended 'sine die'. He was the famed Willie Woodburn.

After signing professional terms in October 1937, having arrived at Ibrox from the juvenile side, Edinburgh Athletic, he made his Rangers debut in the 2-2 game with Motherwell in August 1938. By the end of the Second World War, the No.5 jersey was virtually his, with George Young (another great, natural centre-half) having moved to right-back. Six-foot Woodburn was, indeed, a formidable talent. Whether in the air or on the ground, right foot or left, tackling or passing, there were few signs of weakness in his overall game. He also gave the impression that Rangers were his 'raison d'être' and therefore, little else mattered but success for the club. And success there was in abundance.

A 'double' of League and League Cup in 1946/47 was followed by the Scottish Cup in April 1948. History was in the making the next year, when Rangers became the first team ever to secure a Scottish domestic 'treble' in 1948/49. Twelve months down the line, all three pieces of silverware very nearly stayed in the Ibrox Trophy room but because of defeat at the semi-final stage in the League Cup, Rangers had to make do with just the other two! There was yet another milestone in Season 1950/51, when Willie scored his one and only Rangers goal in the April 3-2 league win over Motherwell. The player completed his personal haul of medals with the duo of League Championship and Scottish Cup in 1952/53.

Woodburn was sent-off for violent conduct near the end of the League Cup fixture against Stirling Albion at Ibrox in late August 1954. It was his fifth red card and, on September 14, 1954, the player was suspended from the game 'sine die'. Although this draconian ban was eventually lifted on 22 April, 1957, his career, by that time, was over. It was a sad end for a hugely talented Rangers man who had worn the dark blue of his country on twenty-four occasions.

After all these years, it is much more fitting that Willie Woodburn be remembered for those special qualities - and there were, indeed, many - that made him such a Rangers giant, rather than for the manner in which his footballing days ended.

Rangers Career Statistics
Games: 325 Goals: 1 League Championship Medals: 4
Scottish Cup Medals: 4 League Cup Medals: 2

CHRIS WOODS

Picture a 'Roy of the Rovers' image of the archetypal English goalkeeper. He would probably be a tall, blond, blue-eyed, muscular, good-looking guy. In other words, a comic-book version of Chris Woods. Rangers had the real thing.

Graeme Souness paid Norwich City a fee of £600,000 in June 1986 for the services of the England No.2 goalkeeper and deputy to Peter Shilton. Considered the best in the country by the Rangers manager, Woods and Terry Butcher (that summer's other essential signing) would become the rocks on which Souness built his Championship side. The manager's faith was more than justified, as the player not only excelled that year but also set a British record of successive games without losing a goal. Beginning with the league visit of Hearts (3-0, 29.11.86) and ending in the Scottish Cup tie at Ibrox against Hamilton (0-1, 3.1.87), Chris Woods played 1196 minutes of football before having to pick the ball out of his own net.

In October of the following season, a contentious 'Old Firm' match at Ibrox (2-2, 17.10.87) saw the 'keeper and his captain, Butcher, along with Celtic's McAvennie, all sent off. The trio plus Graham Roberts (who conducted the Ibrox choir as replacement goalkeeper that day) were later all charged by the police and appeared in court. Due to suspension, Woods missed the League Cup Final against Aberdeen the next weekend but Rangers still lifted the silverware.

Although there was a 'double' of League and League Cup in 1988/89, Chris missed a third of the campaign with a serious virus that affected both his balance and sight.

A damaged shoulder at the start of the following season caused more problems but he played on regardless of the pain. His tally of Scottish medals was completed with another two Championships (1989/90 and 1990/91) and one League Cup (1990/91) before Andy Goram arrived in the summer of 1991. After 230 games for Rangers (and five years at the club), Chris Woods returned south to join Sheffield Wednesday.

His place in the modern Rangers story was assured.

Rangers Career Statistics
Games : 230 Goals : Nil League Championship Medals : 4
League Cup Medals : 3

PETER McCLOY

Certainly, he was tall (all of six feet, four inches) and his birthplace was, indeed, Girvan on the Ayrshire coast. Hardly any surprise, therefore, that a thoughtful fan christened him, 'The Girvan Lighthouse', in a lighthearted moment.

Peter McCloy signed from Motherwell in the spring of 1970, with both Bobby Watson and Brian Heron heading eastwards to Lanarkshire in exchange. His first two games for his new club ('away' to both Dunfermline and Dundee) resulted in 2-1 defeats. Not the best of starts to his Ibrox career. In fact, Rangers only won one of the seven matches that featured him in goal that season! Although McCloy's initial honour with the 'Light Blues' was the League Cup of October 1970 (he kept a 'clean-sheet' in the Final against Celtic), somewhat more prestige was attached to his next medal. In the Barcelona Cup Winners' Cup Final of May 1972, one of his trademark lengthy clearances found Willie Johnston deep in Dynamo territory, enabling the winger to score Rangers' crucial third of the night, prior to the two-goal Russian reply.

A year on, it was the Scottish Cup in that amazing Centenary Final, when Celtic were beaten 3-2. By the time the League Championship arrived back at Ibrox, after eleven long years, in 1975, Stewart Kennedy was the No.1 choice. The two men would alternate in goal for the next three seasons before McCloy claimed the position outright, once again, in 1978/79. Rangers celebrated a 'double' of both domestic Cups that year and 'The Lighthouse' never missed a game. Another two League Cups (1983/84 and 1984/85) followed and with the arrival of Graeme Souness, a new position as goalkeeping coach at the club until 1988.

In the Ibrox hall of fame, Peter McCloy stands tall (!) as Rangers' longest-serving goalkeeper.

Rangers Career Statistics

Games: 535 Goals: 0 League Championship Medals: 1

Scottish Cup Medals: 4 League Cup Medals: 4 European Medals: 1

JIMMY MILLAR

Certain players hold a special place in the hearts of a whole generation of fans. Jimmy Millar is one such individual. Some named the centre-forward 'Warhorse' but his skills belied that badge, as the player was not only fearless and daring but also quite superb in the air, despite being just five-and-a-half feet tall.

Millar was actually a half-back with Dunfermline when Rangers manager, Scot Symon, took him to Ibrox in January 1955 for £5,000. A twist of fate saw a change of team position: due to an injury to Max Murray, Jimmy was moved to centre-forward for the second half of a 'friendly' match against Staevnet in Denmark (May 1959) and promptly scored four. That, as they say, was that!

Many older followers of the team still recall with relish his famous headed goal, from all of sixteen yards, to equalise against Celtic in the 1960 Scottish Cup semi-final. Rangers won the replay 4-1 (with Millar scoring twice) and went on to lift the Cup, defeating Kilmarnock 2-0 in the final with....yes, you've guessed....our man James netting both goals.

The hitman was also top scorer in the league that year, with twenty-one strikes. By Season 1960/61, he had established a deadly partnership with the inimitable Ralph Brand in that great Rangers side of the early sixties. Millar would often win the ball in the air for Brand to convert. Between them, the pair netted over 360 goals for the club. Indeed, it was that very partnership that eventually secured the Scottish Cup of 1964. In a classic final with Dundee, both strikers scored in the last few minutes (for a 3-1 triumph), after Bert Slater had kept them at bay throughout most of the game, performing heroics in the dark blue goal.

In the twilight of his Rangers career, the player collected his fifth Scottish Cup medal, back in his 'old' position of half-back, when Celtic were defeated 1-0 in the April 1966 replay, as Kai Johansen's thunderous shot won the Cup.

Jimmy Millar will forever be remembered as one of the most inspirational centre-forwards to have worn the blue. With pride!

Rangers Career Statistics
Games: 317 Goals: 162 League Championship Medals: 3
Scottish Cup Medals: 5 League Cup Medals: 3

ALAN MORTON

In his time, he was judged to be the finest footballer of a generation. For good reason, therefore, the oil portrait of Alan Morton takes pride of place above the splendid marble stairway inside Ibrox Stadium.

Following his appointment as manager in June 1920, Bill Struth's first signing brought the five foot, four inch, nine-stone winger to the club that same summer from the amateur Queen's Park. Although only a part-time player (with a 'day' job as a mining engineer), his professional contract with Rangers was said to be worth £60 a week. Obviously, a veritable fortune in those days.

Morton had it all, including superb balance and ball control (enabling him to weave and drift past defenders), with a powerful shot in either foot. Although naturally right-footed, he played on the left-wing and for additional mobility, preferred only three studs on each boot as opposed to the normal four. Like David Beckham in the modern game, he could deliver superb crosses that bent and dipped into the box and his 'floating lob' became something of a trademark in the Scottish game. All this, remember, with only a heavy, 'old-fashioned' football at his disposal!

Against Celtic, Morton was a revelation and scored on his 'Old Firm' league debut (in October 1920), when Rangers recorded a 2-1 victory. In that first season of 1920/21, the title was won in some considerable style, with only one defeat along the way. The man himself had style in abundance.

When Scotland crushed England 5-1 in 1928, the 'Wembley Wizards' were born. Morton was sensational that day, with three of his inch-perfect crosses providing the means for Alex Jackson to claim a 'hat-trick'. Seemingly, it was during this game that an exasperated English fan called him a 'Wee Blue Devil'. The name stuck. In all, he wore the dark blue of his country thirty-one times.

1928 was, indeed, a special year for the player. Apart from that memorable victory over the 'Auld Enemy', the winger was part of the emotional Rangers team that lifted the Scottish Cup for the first time in twenty-five years. At Hampden, over 118,000 fans witnessed the famous 4-0 defeat of Celtic. Early-on in Season 1932/33 (after playing seven games), Morton announced his retirement and was immediately made a Rangers director. Over a thirteen year period, he had won two Scottish Cups and an amazing nine League Championships, playing in 440 games and scoring 105 goals.

Alan Morton, just maybe the greatest Ranger of them all, died in 1971......on the same day as another Ibrox legend, Torry Gillick.

Rangers Career Statistics
Games : 440 Goals : 105 League Championship Medals : 9
Scottish Cup Medals : 2

GORDON SMITH

eason 1977/78 had started badly for the 'Light Blues', with defeats at the hands of both Aberdeen (1-3, 13.8.77) and Hibernian (0-2, 20.8.77). One of that summer's fresh arrivals, Davie Cooper, had played in each game but the other newly-signed forward didn't make the starting line-up for either match. One week later, against Partick Thistle at Firhill, Gordon Smith was given his chance and duly scored twice in the 4-0 victory.

In Rangers' next league encounter, it was another 'double', as old rivals, Celtic, fell by three goals to two. Netting a total of eight in his first five Championship games, Smith would go on to record twenty league and six League Cup goals that season. Impressive striking in anyone's book, especially for a player who had actually arrived in Govan (from Kilmarnock) as a winger. His partnership with Derek Johnstone was lethal and the pair claimed sixty-three domestic strikes between them, as Jock Wallace's Rangers raced towards the 'treble', sweeping all before them in a tidal wave of blue.

Although Aberdeen were beaten Scottish Cup finalists in May, it was another game against the 'Granite City' team that drew most applause from supporters and pundits alike. At Ibrox in early October, the 'Dons' were crushed 6-1 in the League Cup, on a day when Rangers were simply awesome. Gordon Smith scored a hat-trick. He would also net, to obvious acclaim, a very late winner in the final of that same competition against Celtic (2-1, 18.3.78). The following season, with John Greig now installed as manager, it was a 'double' of both domestic Cups but no Championship. Just like his great-grandfather before him ('Mattha' Smith of 1920s Kilmarnock), Gordon was now the proud owner of two Scottish Cup medals.

Surprisingly, in 1980, against his own wishes, it must be said, the player was transferred to Brighton. Apart from a brief return in December 1982, his Rangers days were over.

Rangers Career Statistics
Games : 157   Goals : 51   League Championship Medals : 1
Scottish Cup Medals : 2   League Cup Medals 2

JOCK SHAW

It is often said that the modern footballer is far fitter than his counterpart of, say, fifty years ago. Few would argue but of course, there is always an exception. Having lifted the League and Scottish Cup 'double' in 1950 (for the second year in a row), Rangers' captain Jock Shaw, was, understandably, an extremely proud man. He was also thirty-eight years old!

Joining the Ibrox club from Airdrie in July 1938, the player toasted his first Championship the following April, after just one season in Govan. The formation of Rangers' famed 'Iron curtain' defence came about following the end of the Second World War, as football returned to normality and it was in this august line-up (with Brown, Young, McColl, Woodburn and Cox as the other defenders) that Shaw filled the left full-back role. Rangers would go on to win three out of the next four league titles.

An uncompromising tackler (thus the 'Tiger' nickname), the player was so superbly fit that he carried on in the game long after his contemporaries had given up the ghost. In fact, when he did eventually retire after Rangers' 1954 North American Tour (becoming both trainer and groundsman at Ibrox in due course), Shaw was forty-two years old and had accumulated four League, three Scottish Cup and two League Cup medals to place beside his four Scotland 'Caps'.

The Victory Cup of 1946 is one of the few occasions when two brothers have opposed each other in a cup final at Hampden - Jock Shaw was at left-back for Rangers and his brother, David, played in the same position for Hibernian. The pair had actually played together in the Victory International against England (1946), filling the full-back positions for their country. The Easter Road player was later preferred for the No.3 jersey in the national side, thus keeping Jock's tally of Scotland honours to only four.

Brother David may have won that particular family battle but for endurance and lasting quality, a different Shaw comes to mind. And he was a tiger.

Rangers Career Statistics

Games : 283 Goals : 1 League Championship Medals : 4

Scottish Cup Medals : 3 League Cup Medals : 2

GRAHAM ROBERTS

To the 'Bears' of Ibrox, Graham Roberts was, in many ways, the embodiment of all a player should be when he wears the prized blue jersey. Whatever else, the Rangers cause was all that mattered. Maybe that's one of the reasons why, despite less than two seasons at the club, the Englishman is still revered down Govan way.

The defender's 'hard-man' reputation preceded him to Glasgow but in truth, Roberts was much more than just a so-called football heavy. With Tottenham Hotspur in London, he had won not only two FA Cups but also the UEFA Cup in 1984, when Anderlecht were Spurs' final opponents. Roberts actually scored in the second leg against the Belgians. Following a December 1986 transfer, the player's 'Light Blue' debut was against Dundee United in a 2-0 'home' victory. Rangers would then remain unbeaten in the league until early April the next year, four games away from Championship day at Pittodrie. His defensive partnership with Terry Butcher that season was both formidable and inspirational, the two men displaying a blue commitment second to none.

Although Roberts had been sent off against Hamilton in January 1987, the real controversy arose when Celtic came calling on league business some nine months later, in mid October. Following 'keeper Chris Woods' dismissal, the defender pulled on his red jersey and took up position between the posts. At one point in the second half, with the Copland choir in full voice behind him, he conducted them. After the game, he was charged with breach of the peace along with Woods, Butcher and Celtic's McAvennie, all three of whom had been sent off during the game itself. The case against him was eventually ruled 'not proven'.

When Butcher broke his leg against Aberdeen at Ibrox in November 1987, Roberts assumed responsibility as team captain. He had, indeed, been captain for the day when the League Cup was won the previous month at Hampden, against that same team from the 'Granite City'. However, following the second-last game of the season, when Aberdeen won 1-0 at Ibrox, manager Graeme Souness and Roberts 'exchanged words'. His Rangers career effectively over, he joined Chelsea at the beginning of Season 1988/89.

Rangers Career Statistics

Games : 69 Goals : 3 League Championship Medals : 1
League Cup Medals : 1

McEWAN
LAGER